FOLKSONG — PLAINSONG

FOLKSONG — PLAINSONG

A Study in Origins

and

Musical Relationships

by

G. B. CHAMBERS

Preface by

RALPH VAUGHAN WILLIAMS

SECOND EDITION

THE MERLIN PRESS LTD.

11 Fitzroy Square
London, W.1

INSCRIBED

TO THE

MEMORY

OF

TWO FRIENDS

GEORGE H. PALMER and CECIL J. SHARP

Preface

FATHER GEORGE CHAMBERS' masterly treatise ought really to be unnecessary. Hubert Parry in his "Evolution of the Art of Music" has proved conclusively that music obeys the laws of heredity, and that a Beethoven Symphony is in the direct line of descent from a primitive folk song. Surely, what is true in general must be equally true in particular, and the plain song of the church derive from the song of the people.

It is perhaps lucky that our bat-eyed musicologists have not recognised this, and that it has been necessary for Father George Chambers to write this delightful, learned, and, to my mind, entirely persuasive essay. Of course the musicologists cannot altogether ignore the connection between plain song and folk song, but they have put the cart before the horse and imagine that the music of the people is the debased descendant of that of the church. In their opinion the written word was impeccable and oral tradition fallible. But in truth the clerk may make errors in his copying while the memory of the unlettered countryman is sure.

One of the most interesting chapters of this book contains convincing proof that the "Jubilus" is not an ecclesiastical parallel to the coloratura of the prima donna, but has developed out of the wordless melismata of primitive people when their mystical emotions got beyond words. This is only one instance of the deep research and thorough scholarship which pervades the book.

RALPH VAUGHAN WILLIAMS

CONTENTS

Introduction

THE following treatise is the outcome of many years study and consideration of the relation between Folksong and the Plainsong of the Church. At first it seemed that the kinship might lie rather through the survival in the minds of the people of musical themes once known and loved in the Services of the Church—the musical remnants of past ages—than through the Church adopting the musical methods of the folk. In the first instance the writer offered his theory with some doubt and trepidation, but further study, and the appearance of a considerable amount of literature, both directly and indirectly bearing on the whole subject, has shown definite confirmation for the position now taken up.

The Ecclesiastical Chant at the beginning, whether melismatic or syllabic, can be found in the musical customs and methods of the people. Important patristic references to the "Jubilation" can be found in the writings of S. Augustine, S. John Chrysostom, S. Isidore of Seville, S. Hilary and one invaluable reference as far back as Clement of Alexandria. All these quotations have immediate reference to the songs of the people. Referring to the mystical significance of the "Jubilation", comparison is drawn with later writers, such as Richard Rolle and S. Teresa. There is also a passage in the *Summa* of S. Thomas Aquinas on rhythmical movement which deserves careful analysis. The whole question of the "quality" of rhythm is dealt with in a special section. I have also had access to two interesting works by the late Dr. Steiner on *Eurhythmy as Visible Speech* and *Eurhythmy as Visible Song*.

My indebtedness and thanks to former teachers, friends and writers is almost beyond calculation and first and foremost I must mention the Father Abbot of Prinknash Abbey, Gloucester, and those of his brethren, who in the days that are now long past learnt with me the spiritual value and meaning of the chant and "Quocum dulce habui consortium, in domo Dei ambulavimus in coetu festivo." Ways may divide, but time can never blot out the memory of experiences, the value of which abides for ever. I have to thank Mrs. A. M. Adam of Cambridge for the care and trouble she took in tracing for me the use and significance of "Jubilatio" in Classical Latin. To Father Lewis Andrews, S.S.M., and the Rev. R. C. Walls for help and criticism in the chapter dealing with Vernacular Rites, and especially to the latter for the entire note on the Hebrew and Greek equivalents of the "Jubilatio". I am also grateful to Mr. Peter Crossley-Holland for useful information about Welsh Homophonic Music and its possible bearing on the notational evolution of the chant. I must extend my gratitude, too, to Miss Dorothy Smith who has ably assisted me when lecturing by her vocal illustrations of the melismatic and syllabic chant as well as by her attractive rendering of the folksongs. I must also mention Mr. and Mrs. H. McClatchey who sent me useful information on two important questions which required elucidation. On the side of folksong and folkdance, I am equally indebted to my friends and co-workers in the English Folk Dance and Song Society; especially my old friend Miss Maud Karpeles and the former librarian at Cecil Sharp House, Miss Margaret Dean-Smith. When I think how far my interest extends back more than forty years, to the days when my late friend Conrad Noel and his wife Miriam began their work at Thaxted, it may be both expedient and fitting that my own small contribution and effort in this direction should be recorded, if only in gratitude to those friends, living and departed, with whom I have shared this experience.

More recently my indebtedness has turned to America, now alas to the late Dr. George Pullen Jackson and his considerable catalogue of invaluable books, and to others whom I have named in the course of my essay. This "American tradition" has been indispensable in determining a final conclusion in the main theme of this work. I therefore gratefully record my thanks to the above author for his advice and readiness to correspond with me on the various issues which have arisen.

G. B. C.
CARBROOKE, 1955.

CHAPTER I

Patristic Testimony

Patristic Testimony

In approaching the question of the origin of any form of musical art it is difficult to prevent our pre-suppositions from colouring, not only the line of our study, but also the conclusions we may draw from our researches. In the course of the centuries musical technique has changed very considerably; therefore, before we can trace back and discover the situation in its initial stages, we must put out of mind our own present-day background and try to picture a world, without printing, when Greek and Latin were the predominant languages, when the capacity to write was limited, and when great social changes were taking place through the spread of the Christian faith and the · insecurity arising from external invasion. In the fourth and fifth centuries, there was no musical technique in the sense that the ninth century acquired a technique and musical notation. Furthermore the eleventh century was better served with the development of technical musical form than the previous centuries. Whether the study of musical art was really advanced by these changes is another matter; the changes arose in response to certain needs which were often bound up with the history and circumstances affecting European culture generally, and the evolution of individual nations. In the tradition both of the Folksong and Plainsong, memory plays a very important part. Investigation has shown how persistent and accurate are the memories of unlettered folk; apparently, reading and writing lessen the power of the memory. Now in an age devoid of printing, the capacity to remember represents the centre and kernel of tradition, manuscripts were few and the words of the text of Holy Scripture, for instance, had to be committed to memory; just as the songs of the people were learnt and handed on through the generations. It seems almost absurd to point out that all the paraphernalia of modern musical accompaniment was lacking, but to clear our background, it is necessary to emphasize this particular feature in order to understand the wide gap between ancient and modern musical practice. We want to discover what happened in the beginning, when the Church was trying to reshape the world of human affairs, and re-form the culture of Greece and Rome, essentially "religious" in its foundation and still representing the ancient fertility rites and customs of the people. The world at large certainly understood the meaning of "worship", but the Church challenged, not only the source, but the object and direction of man's homage in relation to God. What then did happen? It is not difficult to trace the "shape" of the primitive Liturgy, but to work out anything relating to exact detail is quite another matter —"singing" is one of the details in question; singing is important because it accompanies worship. Where the soul of man is lifted up in worship, the expression of the soul through the singing voice is certain to be present; worship, prayer and singing are very closely allied, if not actually identical.

The question now arises, if people were singing at the beginning of the Christian Era, what was the form and theme of their song and the occasion of its expression. Is there evidence to show that men, women and children sang while at their work for instance? Is it possible for us today to picture conditions of life completely different from our own? Have the outstanding personalities of the Church, whose writings survive, left us any useful information? To every one of these questions an affirmative answer may be given. Theologians, like Clement of Alexandria, S. Augustine, S. John Chrysostom, S. Isidore of Seville, S. Jerome, Cassiodorus, and others, give us definite information. They tell us the folk of their day were a singing people, they sang at their work, they found joy in singing, and what is more, the theme and method of their vocalisation was carefully observed by these self-same men whose writings have come down to us.

Clement of Alexandria, towards the end of the second century, writes words of warning about behaviour at feasts and convivial gatherings. (Paedagogus Lib. II, Ch. IV).

"Modest and pure singing ought to be allowed : on the other hand too energetic rendering, however lengthy, ought to be spurned, which leads to wanton effeminacy and scurrility by a doubtful artificial turn of the voice. But sombre and modest jubilations dismiss the messenger of wanton drunkenness. Therefore wanton songs are to be left to the intoxicated and garlanded and to the music of the courtesan."

At a very early stage we have here, not a condemnation of singing, or of convivial entertainment, but very definite strictures on the form and range of the melody and the words which

3

accompany it, and a distinct feeling that certain musical intervals (chromaticae harmoniae) are not a desirable medium for the expression of Christian joy. The method, with reservations, is approved, but care and discretion must be adopted in its use. It is also important to note the words Clement uses with approval : "Graves . . . modulationes." Without hesitation I have translated "modulatio" as "jubilation" because it is not only melody but a very distinct melodic form. I hope this rendering will be justified as the work proceeds.

Turning to S. Augustine (d. 430) the whole question of singing in relation to the Liturgy is very considerably clarified. S. Augustine, in his commentary on the Psalms, has written at some length on the meaning and force of singing "In jubilatione". Commenting on Psalm 32 he writes : "Notice the method of singing he gives you, don't look for words that you may be able, as it were, to explain how God is pleased : sing a 'Jubilation'. What does singing a 'Jubilation' mean? It is the realisation that words cannot express the inner music of the heart. For those who sing in the harvest field, or vineyard, or in work deeply occupying the attention, when they are overcome with joy at the words of the song, being filled with such exultation, the words fail to express their emotion, so, leaving the syllables of the words, they drop into vowel sounds— the vowel sounds signifying that the heart is yearning to express what the tongue cannot utter."

And again commenting on Psalm 99 he says : "A man who sings a 'jubilation' does not use words because 'a jubilation' is the expression of joy without words . . . a man singing in the joy of his own heart bursts forth into (vowel) sounds when normal means of utterance fail to express his meaning. Thus it is apparent that a man is vocally expressing joy, although being overcome by his joyfulness, he cannot explain in words why he rejoices."

The following statement occurs on Psalm 97 : "Jubilate Deo" : "You know already what it is to sing a jubilation, rejoice and speak. If you cannot express your joy, let the jubilation do it, what is more expressive of joy than the jubilation? If speech is not expressive, joy need not therefore be silent." *

It is evident from these statements that this method of singing, which has left such an impression on the worship of the Church, was a well-known folk practice and strikingly noticed by the observant mind of S. Augustine. There is no suggestion in his

---

* For the purpose of translation and interpretation it is important to notice S. Augustine's use of the term "sonus." He refers to it as identical with "jubilatio" in "sonum" jubilationis. We shall see that S. Isidore of Seville used "sonus" with a similar meaning.

comments that it was the result of distinctively Christian aspiration, but rather the expression of the emotion of the ordinary peasant folk while engaged in their daily toil. But at the same time, transferred to Catholic worship and prayer, it has at once an enhanced value, it is the expression of the soul in the higher sense, it ceases to be merely a subconscious utterance and becomes part of the spirit's yearning for the inner things of God.

The word jubilatio seems to convey this idea, it is a term used, not only in a Christian, but in a distinctively mystical sense. Witness S. Augustine again explaining the meaning of the words "Ascendit Deus in jubilatione" (Psalm 46). "What is a jubilation save the exuberance of joy which words cannot explain." And on Psalm 44. "Jubilemus Deo salutari nostro," he writes, "What is a jubilation? Joy not to be expressed in words, yet the voice bears witness to what is conceived within and what cannot be explained verbally (when sung) this is a jubilation. For let your charity consider those who in certain songs and, as it were, in a certain striving for worldly pleasure, jubilate (sing on vowel sounds) and you see, as it were in the songs expressed by the words an overflowing joy, where speech is not sufficient, so they break into singing on vowel sounds, that through this means the feeling (affectus) of the soul may be described, words failing to explain what the heart conceives. Therefore, if they (folksingers) jubilate from earthly exhilaration, ought not we to sing the jubilation through heavenly joy, what words cannot articulate." Perhaps this is the most definite statement he makes on the whole matter, he not only mentions it as a folk custom, but notes its transference to Christian worship because it was derived from a subconscious source and could therefore be made to fulfil a much higher spiritual need and yearning.

Before we proceed from the West to the East and examine confirmatory evidence from S. John Chrysostom, it may be well to turn again to S. Augustine, to Ch. 7, Bk. 9, of the Confessions, because this particular passage denotes the spiritual and physical crisis which called forth a particular change in the rendering of the Divine Office.

S. Augustine asserts that the custom of singing hymns and psalms in church grew up in the Western Empire on a very distinct occasion. He refers to the troubles which arose owing to the controversy between the Empress Justina and S. Ambrose at Milan, how his own mother kept nightly vigil in the church on behalf of their beloved bishop, Ambrose.

"Thence the custom arose of singing hymns and psalms after the manner of the Easterns, lest the people might be depressed

5

by the weight of their grief and from that time up to today the custom has been retained, many already, if not all Thy congregations through the rest of the world, following the example."

* * * *

Turning to an Eastern theologian, S. John Chrysostom writes a note on Psalm 41 : "Therefore it is first necessary to explain the reason why the Psalm has been brought into our life and with singing this is especially called prophecy."* "On this account therefore it may be said, attend with song."

"Since God, having seen that many men were more foolish and did not approach freely to the reading of things spiritual, and that a man, who is occupied therewith is apt to lose interest, desiring to make the work more attractive, and to open out the sense of it, He added melody to prophecy that all men charmed by the inflection (modulatione) of the singing, with great readiness of soul may send forth holy hymns to Him. For nothing fitly lifts up the soul, and influences it in such a manner when exalted, frees it from earth and looses it from the burden of the flesh, affects it with the love of wisdom that everything belonging to this life may flourish and be perfect, as the singing of musical intervals,† divine song well ordered. Our nature surely is so constantly delighted with songs and melodies that infants at the breast, if they cry and are troubled are soothed in this way; nurses certainly who carry infants in arms, going to and fro often, are singing to them childrens' ditties and keep them quiet in this way. Moreover travellers in the middle of the day, making a journey on yoked animals, sing, finding consolation from the tedium of the journey in these songs. And not only travellers but farm workers treading the grapes in the wine press, gathering the grapes, or training the vines, and doing any other work whatsoever, frequently sing. Sailors as well, when rowing, do this. Women also while weaving, and when separating a tangled warp on the beam, sometimes individually, at other times all together, sing one particular melody.

"And since filth attracts pigs, and sweet smells and perfumes bees, so, where gross songs are sung, there evil influences are pre-

---

* For scriptural explanation see 1 Chronicles, 25, 1-7.

† The Latin rendering is " Cantus modulationis," the Greek has ὡς μέλος δυμφωίας

It appears that modulatio is used in the same sense and with the same meaning as jubilatio, the practice of singing a long musical phrase on a vowel sound mentioned by S. Augustine and Clement of Alexandria. See also the Rule of S. Benedict, Ch. 18 (p. 81, Solesmes ed.), " Vespera autem quotidie quattuor Psalmorum modulatione canatur." See also Wagner's *Hist. of Plainchant*, p. 28, et passim, for an examination of John Cassian's testimony in reference to the same matter.

sent, but where there are spiritual songs thither the grace of the Spirit hastens, which sanctifies the mouth and the soul. I say this, not that you only may sing praise, but that you may teach your sons and wives to sing such songs, not only when weaving and doing other work, but especially at the table. For the devil is very much on the lookout at feasts for drunkenness, gluttony and uproarious laughter and when souls are off their guard, then it is very greatly necessary, both before and after meals, to fortify oneself with the protection of the Psalter, and likewise with wife and children rising from dinner to sing holy hymns to God."

I do not think anyone would care to deny the importance of this evidence. Two outstanding personalities, S. Augustine and S. John Chrysostom, in their commentaries on the psalms, mention in some detail what were the manners and customs of people when singing, and the exact circumstances of their songs. There was much in the words they sang which was considered unworthy of Christians, therefore the music ought to be used, but allied with the words of the psalter, because the psalms were the centre and soul of Christian worship and the inspiration of Christian life. We cannot help noticing the emphasis laid on the distinctive method, singing "In Jubilatione" or "Modulatione"—this was applied to the psalms and became known in the Church as the "Responsorial Chant". Today we call it very "elaborate" singing, but the practice was so widespread at the time of the expansion of the liturgy in the fourth century that, what would have seemed impossible to modern musical capacity, represented no difficulty to the congregations of the Primitive Church. Witness the testimony of Cassiodorus in his commentary on the Psalms, where he used a similar method of interpretation to S. Augustine's "Enarrationes". Writing of the Alleluia he says: "This is dedicated to the Churches of God, this is fitly appropriate to the holy festivals; on the one side it adorns the tongue of the cantors, on the other the congregation joyfully answer and, like something good of which one can never have enough, in ever varying jubilations it is renewed." Cassiodorus lived and wrote between 490-583 A.D., rather late in the formative period of the liturgy, so it seems fairly evident the ordinary folk at the end of the sixth century were taking active part in the melismatic or responsorial chant.*

---

* "Hoc ecclesiis Dei votivum, hoc sanctis festivitatibus decenter accommodatum. Hinc ornatur lingua cantorum: istud aula domini laeta respondet et tamquam insatiabile bonum, tropis semper variantibus innovatur." (Cassiodorus in Psalm 104. Patr. Lat. 735). For reasons for translating "tropis" here by "jubilations" or "melismata" see Wagner's *Hist. of Plainchant* (pp. 28 ff.). He writes: "It can only mean the singing of an elaborate musical phrase."

It appears unnecessary, but I feel rather bound to remind anyone reading these pages that printed hymn books were not in the hands of the congregations referred to by Cassiodorus. After centuries of "print" our preconceived notions become so set, a reminder about primitive conditions of worship becomes imperative. Surely it is obvious that the contemporaries of Cassiodorus sang in a musical theme with which they were quite familiar. As Christians, worship was their chief interest in life; whether they were lettered or unlettered, they knew their psalms.

Before discussing the further uses and references to the "Jubilatio", it may be well to give the testimony of another Latin Doctor, S. Jerome. Writing about Psalm 32 he refers to the "jubilus" or jubilation[*]—"That is called jubilus which neither in words, nor syllables, nor letters, nor in speech, can utter or define how much man ought to praise God." No doubt S. Jerome had this interpretation of the word in his mind when he used "jubilare" in his translations of the Psalter.

* * * *

The testimony of S. Isidore deserves a separate study because his method of treatment is distinctive and his statements, in one direction at all events, conclusive. S. Isidore draws a contrast between "sonus" and "cantus"; the former he uses to describe the jubilation and the latter refers to what we might call more straightforward ways of singing. He writes: "Without Music there can be no perfect knowledge, without it knowledge is nothing. For the world also to be rightly ordered revolves in a certain harmony of sound, and heaven functions under the rhythm of the jubilation (sub harmonia modulatione). Music influences the affections and stimulates the feelings in various ways.

"In warfare too the sound of the trumpet fires the combatants : and the more vehement the sound so much the more the soul is strengthened for the fight. In the same way, singing encourages the oarsmen. For making work lighter music soothes the mind, the rise and fall of the voice (modulatio vocis) eases the fatigue arising from each task.

---

[*] Jubilus dicitur, quod nec verbis, nec syllabis nec litteris nec voce potest erumpere aut comprehendere quantum homo Deum debeat laudare (Patr Lat. xxvi, 970, Migne).

"Tonal movement (Harmonia) is the jubilation of the voice (the melismatic chant), the concord or the accurate joining together* of very many intervals of sound.

"Singing is an inflection of the voice, for sonus is the flow of rhythm (directus est)."† "Sonus comes before cantus." That is, the jubilation, or singing on a vowel sound, has preceded vocal utterance where words are used, sonus is therefore the easy ordered flow of melody which is associated with the "melisma", cantus the inflection of the voice in ordered expression.

Before dealing with a further passage of S. Isidore it may be well to consider the background, as far as dates are concerned, of the personalities whose testimony we have referred to at some length. S. John Chrysostom and S. Augustine were contemporary, both lived in the middle of the fourth century and died in the fifth. S. Isidore (b cir. 570, d. 636), was a younger contemporary of S. Gregory who was born circa 540 and died 604. Cassiodorus was born circa 490 and probably died 583.

S. John Chrysostom and S. Augustine would have witnessed the liturgical changes which accompanied the altered policy of the Roman Empire towards the Christian Faith under Constantine. To a certain extent this formative period was drawing to a close by the time of S. Gregory.

What was the liturgical inheritance, particularly in regard to singing which S. Gregory handed on? The tradition is fairly fixed that he was a reformer, so at the beginning of the seventh century we may have a distinct attempt at the hands of S. Gregory to introduce some system of standardization. Speaking quite broadly, the text of the liturgy having its source in the psalms and

---

* Co-aptatio=an accurate joining together. A word coined by S. Augustine for translating the Greek ἁρμονία Aug: Trin: 4.2 and Civ: Dei 22.24 (Dict: Lewis & Short). In 22.24 of the *De Civitate* S. Augustine mentions medical practice when dissecting, the separation of limbs in order to see the "co-aptatio" or "harmonia" of the body. S. Augustine describing in his inimitable terse phraseology the scheme of redemption, writes: "Haec enim congruentia sive *convenientia* vel *concinentia* vel *consonantia* vel si quid commodius dicitur, quod unum est ad duo in omni compaginatione vel si melius dicitur, coaptatione creaturae, valet plurimum. Hanc enim coaptationem sicut mihi nunc occurrit, dicere volui, quam Graeci ἁρμονίαν vocant."

† S. Isidore's use of "directus" may serve to elucidate the meaning of "in directum" in the 12th Chapter of the Rule of S. Benedict. If "directus" has this meaning in the "Rule", then the 66th Psalm would certainly not have been rendered without chant. See illuminating articles in *Pax* on the "Origins of the Monastic Office", by Father John Morson, O.C.R. (No. 239) where this writer points out that "In directum" does not exclude melody, and if the above interpretation of S. Isidore holds good, would be far removed from what, in modern parlance, is called monotone.

other passages from Holy Scripture had been established more or less, at the earliest period of the Christian era, but the music was evidently traditional and subject to no definite musical rule or notation. Has enough evidence been produced in this essay already to show where the origin of the Catholic chant is to be found? Surely in the song of the people, the folksong, as it is aptly described. The Fathers of the Church were surrounded by a singing people, their melodies had given inspiration to their lives. For generations and generations this same phenomenon had taken place, but since the words accompanying the singing were unworthy of Christians, henceforward the divine words of the Holy Scriptures must be substituted for the debased words of their former songs, and when they jubilate in exhilaration, as Clement of Alexandria emphasised, they must be sober, not drunk, and not give vent to the phallic utterances of the courtesan. Even if the source of the chant is to be found in a Roman, Greek, Hebrew tradition, where did the said tradition spring from among these three nationalities? There were no printed text books to consolidate a universal method of singing, such preconceptions and suppositions are the result of our modern background, which has no connection with the state and condition of the primitive Christian ages. Christian men and women sang in the theme and manner familiar to them, as S. Augustine and S. John Chrysostom tell us. Books and documents were unnecessary since singing "in jubilatione" was common the world over amongst the folk. If the fathers and theologians of the Primitive Church encouraged their congregations to sing in the mode and manner they knew, we can hardly be surprised that the same method has been adopted throughout the ages down to the beginning of the nineteenth century, often under vastly changed conditions compared with early times.*

---

* *Vid.* Ch. x. *"The American Tradition".*

CHAPTER 1

NOTE I

THIS note deals with N.T. references to singing.—Ep : Colos :
3-16 and Ephes : 5-19 and also Pliny's statement about the
Christian Assembly in letter 90 of his correspondence with the
Emperor Trajan.

The quotations are—"Teaching and admonishing yourselves
in psalms, hymns, spiritual songs, singing, in grace in your heart
to God"—(Col : 3-16) and — "Speaking to yourselves in psalms,
hymns, spiritual songs, singing and making melody in your heart
to the Lord" (Ephes : 5-19).

Dr. Egon Wellesz (Hist. of Byzantine Music, Clarendon Press,
Ch : 1, p. 33) considers that the significant words in these passages
"correspond to actual liturgical usages, and that the Christians to
whom the Epistles were addressed would have understood the meaning of each term and have been able to differentiate between them."
But when we study the whole Chapter in both instances, surely
we cannot be too certain at this remote period about "actual
liturgical usages". These very words seem to suggest more settled
customs. Examine both chapters, especially Colossians Ch. iii,
where these words form the climax to the opening verse. "If then
ye were raised together with Christ, seek the things which are
above. . . ." It is a life of "rapture" which the Apostle looks for,
quite possibly acquired through the ecstatic medium of the "jubilation", but at the most we can only urge this explanation as a
remote probability. To state definitely that the "spiritual songs"
of which S. Paul speaks were obviously the melismatic melodies
of the Alleluias and other exultant songs of praise, which is the
contention of Dr. Wellesz (op. cit. p. 33), is clearly drawing a
conclusion which is not permissible from the actual evidence. It
may also be well to refer to the incident in Acts : 16-25 when Paul
and Silas.chained in prison and "praying were singing (hymnoun)
to God" and apparently amazing phenomena followed from their
action.

The present writer reviewed at some length Dr. Egon Wellesz's
History of Byzantine Music in *Music and Letters* (Jan. 1950). I
look upon this work as an invaluable contribution to the study of
Musical origins, but I am truly surprised when Dr. Wellesz passes
over and does not even mention Folksong in relation to this matter.
He refers to Professor Idelsohn as the chief authority on the
Jewish tradition and yet this musician points out that the source
of Jewish Music is Folksong from beginning to end. This fact must
be kept in mind when considering the Old Testament as the
inspired writings of the Catholic Church as well as the Synagogue.

If printing had been in existence, together with formal musical technique which Jewish Rabbis, or more appropriately, the "Chazzanim" would have handed to the Christian Cantors in order that the latter might carry forward a settled method of chanting, the source and origin of the Chant might have been a straightforward matter to decide. But such a situation did not exist. Therefore, it is hardly a justifiable conclusion to urge, when S. Isidore of Seville describes the Alleluia as a Hebrew canticle, that the Christians waited on Jews to be taught how to sing it. S. Isidore actually wrote "Laudes, hoc est Alleluia Canere; anticum est Hebraeorum". "The Praises, that is to sing the Alleluia, is a canticle of the Jews". I give a literal, but surely, an intelligible translation of the actual text. Idelsohn, apparently relying on the authority of Peter Wagner, translates the passage—"The tunes of Laudations, that is Halleluyah-singing, is of Hebrew origin." I venture to consider this translation of a straightforward Latin sentence as a decidedly tendentious rendering. The Alleluia and other Hebrew words occur continually in Catholic liturgical texts but surely this does not permit us to imply or jump to the conclusion that the Catholic chant which accompanied the Hebrew words in Catholic Assemblies followed a "set" Jewish pattern. Another fragment with a very primitive connection is found at the beginning of the second century in the 90th letter of Pliny to the Emperor Trajan. This letter describes Pliny's attitude to the Christians. The point of interest to us arises out of the reference to Christian observances and especially to religious worship. The sentence is—"Quod essent soliti stato die ante lucem convenire carmenque Christo quasi deo dicere." These words can be translated—"That they (the Christians) were accustomed on an appointed day very early to assemble together and to hold a service to Christ as God."

It is extraordinary the use which has been made out of the two words "carmen" and "dicere". They have often been quoted to "prove" that Christians at this period sang their liturgy. Singing may or may not have accompanied their worship but dicere carmen in all probability refers to a "set form of words". At all events there is little justification for Dr. Wellesz's contention that of course Christians sang at their assemblies because Pliny uses these two descriptive words in that particular sense, whereas they are equally open to a different interpretation. Pliny may well mean "to hold a service" and nothing more in this official report. The whole question is ably discussed in a note to a small volume of Pliny's Letters edited by C. E. Prichard and E. R. Bernard (Clarendon Press). These editors point out that "carmen" here is "not necessarily either lengthy or metrical. All that 'carmen' implies is 'a set form of words'." (Pliny Ep : 90, Pt. ii, p. 65, notes op. cit.). Furthermore, Canon J. H. Shrawley refers ("Early Hist. of the Liturgy," p. 30) to Newman who renders the passage "saying with one another a form of words (carmen) to Christ as if to a God."

(Essay on Development, ch. VI) Canon Shrawley also quotes the late Dom Connolly who considered the sentence to mean "to repeat amongst themselves an invocation to Christ". Lightfoot comments on Pliny's use of "carmenque"—"the word does not necessarily imply a metrical composition but is used of any set form of words." (Vide Apostolic Fathers, pt. ii, p. 51, note on Pliny's letter.)

It is, however, quite true that Tertullian (Apologeticus adv. Gentes, Ch. ii, p. 321, Migne Tomus Prior) when quoting in his own words this particular passage from Pliny's letter used the words "ad canendum Christo ut Deo". But here again, "canere" has diverse meanings. Migne's Lexicon has an interesting description, "Canere—to recite secretly—the custom has arisen in the Church that a supplication (obsecratio) and a consecration may be said (canatur) silently that so sacred words be not used irreverently. It is used about certain words which contain and indicate descriptive quality such as the French say 'Que Chante ce livre', meaning by the use of 'chante', what does this book embrace". (What is the subject matter of this book?—translation from Migne's Lexicon. Vide Infra).

If due consideration is given to the various authorities quoted, it is surely advisable, as already suggested, not to arrive at too hasty conclusions about the meaning and import of a single Latin sentence in an endeavour to establish a definite theory in regard to the particular customs surrounding primitive Christian worship.

Lexicon Manuale ad Scriptores Mediae et Infimiae Latinitatis, Migne. Canere—Privatim recitare; Venit consuetudo in Ecclesia ut tacite obsecratio a sacerdote canatur, ut verba tam sacra vilescerent. (Remig. Antissiod Monach.) Dicitur de litteris quidpiam continentibus et indicantibus qualiter etiamnum Galli dicunt: "Que Chante ce livre"? Quid canit hoc est quod complecitur hic liber?

Tertullian. Apologeticas adv : Gentes (Ch. ii, p. 321, Migne tomus prior)—

"Plinius enim Secundus (38) cum provinciam regeret, damnatis quibusdam Christianis, quibusdam gradu pulsis (39) ipsa tamen multitudine perturbatus, quid de caetero ageret, consuluit tunc Trajanum imperatorem allegans praeter obstinationem non sacrificandi nichil aluid se de sacramentis eorum comperisse quam coetus ante lucanos ad canendum Christo ut Deo. . . ."

BOETHIUS DE MUSICA. (c. 480-524)

Although instruments and acoustics are not actually within the scope of this treatise, yet interest seems to be increasing in the work and knowledge of the ancient Greeks in relation to their theory of music. An article has appeared in "Dominican Studies" (Vol. IV, 1951) on "St. Thomas Aquinas and Music" by Fr. Sebastian Bullough, O.P. This essay deals with the ancient theory of acoustics and harmony and also its psychological effect. Fr. Sebastian shows that the statements made by St. Thomas in the De Anima and the Summa are based on the much earlier treatise of Boethius De Musica and also on St. Augustine's work which bears the same title—De Musica. Professor Farrington's excellent two volumes on Greek Science (Pelican Series) has briefly, but quite effectively, dealt with the same matter from the Greek angle. The latter is the most intelligible from the more popular standpoint but Fr. Sebastian's article, while more technical, represents an invaluable contribution to the whole subject.

As I have suggested the use or the science of musical instruments, much less the extremely technical character of the theories which the Greeks wove round their experience in these matters, is not within our purview. The rhythm of sound and the movements relating to it, in other words the science of acoustics was a metaphysical as well as a physical form of expression to the philosophers of this wonderful nation.

In the treatise of Boethius on Music you find the full Greek tradition described with all its analytical abstruseness and allied with Geometry and Mathematics but, Book 1, Ch. 34, comes rather suddenly within our sphere with the heading, "Quid sit Musicus"—What is a musician? I proceed to give a translation of the entire passage (Bk. 1. Ch. 34, Vol. 63, p. 1195)—

"We must now consider what art really is, all knowledge naturally has a more honourable basis than craftsmanship which is effected by the hand and work of the artificer. For it is much greater and higher to think out what each one shall do than to put his knowledge into effect himself; for material craftsmanship, by performing a service, is a slave to that service. But reason like an Empress bears sway and unless what the hand does is controlled by reason it acts in vain.

"How much more outstanding is the knowledge of music when guided by reason than merely in action and effect as if bodily action was superior to its mental impulse. Hence it is clear without the reasoning faculty, a man lives in servitude, reason indeed is supreme and is conducive to a right attitude, which unless he is obedient to its sway, the work will be a "stammering" without sense. Whence it comes about that speculation is not wanting in the course of rational operation, there may be no manual action except by the use of mental process. Already how great is the glory and merit of reason can now be understood, because for the rest (as I say) it is not from knowledge material works arise but rather from the instruments themselves that the descriptions have their beginning. For the harpist from the harp or the flautist from the flute and the rest of them are called by the names of their own instruments. He is truly a musician who, with all reasonable consideration, gains knowledge of music not by mechanical operation but by the power of thought, knowledge of singing not in the spirit of servitude but dominated by the spirit of discovery. We notice this feature in the works of architecture and Generalship or maybe in popular tradition. For their names are either inscribed on the buildings or they are led in triumph, whose dominion has been rationally established and not made perfect by uninspired servitude. There are, therefore, three features which belong to the art of music : the kind which is governed by instruments, the second composes songs (or poems), the third which pronounces judgment of the work of the instrumentalist and the poet. But the work of the instrumentalist really embraces the whole position, such as the harpists. All harpists by their instruments prove their worth to all the rest of the musical instruments, the harpists have been separated from the understanding of musical science because they are in service (as it is said); they have not brought reason to bear and are wholly without the educated mind. Secondly indeed it is the "Poets" (genus poetarum) who make music effective, because music is here introduced by natural instinct rather than by speculation or reason and therefore this (poetic) group must be separated from actual music. Thirdly skilled judgment comes in when a man is able to weigh carefully the rhythm of the folksongs (cantilenasque) and (decide) their musical value (Carmen).

Because it is clear when the whole has been put to the test of reason and speculation, this may be appropriately esteemed the art of music. He is a musician then who has the capacity to explain according to what is laid down by speculation and reason and consonant with the musical art, the modes and rhythms as applied to the various types of folksongs (deque generibus Cantilenarum), and concerning the thorough mixing together of all those matters which must be explained hereafter and about the songs of the poets (this matter) at its very beginning is a unity or else it is nothing."

It is clear that the foregoing statement certainly contains characteristics of the "Greek View of Life". It may be well as far as possible to consider the connotation of important words which occur frequently.—"Ratio"—reason; this word implies more than reasonableness—it is not only the intellectual and ratiocinative faculty but also the spiritual impulse inspiring it. "Speculatio" —speculation is the analytical and dialectical process whereby a thesis is advanced, defended or criticised. This may explain the somewhat drastic conclusion that servitude precludes true artistic self-expression. The instrumentalists were evidently looked upon as following a pattern, the real artist was the designer, the composer. A point of view which would find little response today. The whole situation reflects the social order of classical times. However, Boethius is more in line with his near contemporaries, St. Augustine and St. John Chrysostom, in his treatment of "cantilenae", the songs of the People, the Folksongs—he evidently felt like the great theologians already mentioned that the foundation of art music is amongst the Folk. I do not think any other conclusion or interpretation can be drawn from the Latin statement. For the rest, what Boethius alleges about his work is emphatically true, the "thorough mixing together" (de permixtioribus) of mathematics, geometry, scales, and modes with an equally thorough metaphysical analysis of the whole system. Small wonder that Christian moral theologians were doubtful about instrumental accompaniment in the worship of the Church; the human voice unaccompanied was more Soulful and therefore less complicated. I should also venture to allege that this instrumental art of the Greeks was deeply imbedded in the Folksongs but the whole situation has no great relation with the work of the Composer in the later ages.

At the same time, it is curious how long musical theory continued to be "mixed up" with geometry and mathematics, clearly the result of the study of Boethius' De Musica.

Before leaving this matter, it may be well to offer further justification for translating "Cantilena" as Folksong in the modern sense of the word. As far as I have been able to discover Boethius uses the word eight times : Viz. "Hence is it that a sweet cradle song (Cantilena dulcis) delights infants." Boethius (op. Cit :) Ch. i, p. 1171.

"Why, because when anyone receives a folksong more freely by spiritual and aural contact, he is not drawn to it spontaneously that the body may express some emotion like the folksong he has heard but because the soul itself gathers up a memory of the sweetness it has received?" (ibid ut supra)

". . . that there may be no age (or condition) altogether separated from the joy of a sweet folksong." (Bk. 1, p. 1168).

"Moreover it is common knowledge how often a folksong will repress outbursts of temper" (p. 1170). . . . "That they might resolve certain daily cares in sleep some people use folksongs that to them a light and quiet slumber might ensue." (infra p. 1170)

". . . and the first is mundane, the second human, the third that which in certain instruments has been established in the lyre or in the pipes which are handmaids to the folksong." (Ch. ii, p. 1174).

"Thus it is not sufficient for the folksongs to delight the musicians let it be realised unless by such a method they may be united by the comparative relation of the voices." (Ch. ii, p. 1171)

Bk. 1, Ch. xxi, p. 1188, deals with the kinds of folksongs but diverges into types of melodies or tunes "de generibus melorum".

All these quotations and references are interesting since they illustrate the source of the melodies on which Boethius built up his complicated musical technique—"Cithara and tibia" are the "handmaids" and therefore dependent on this primary foundation the "Cantilena", a body of song inherent in the human soul and not necessarily contingent on the hand of the harpist or the purely physical skill of the flautist. The impulse began in the subconscious, developed through the imagination to its full fruition in the life and circumstances of each individual.

Considering the many patristic statements already given surely the source of primitive melodies cannot be seriously questioned?

LATIN TEXT—BOETHIUS DE MUSICA. P. MIGNE, VOL. 63, P. 1195.

Nunc illud est intuendum quod omnis ars, omnisque etiam disciplina honorabiliorem naturaliter habent rationem, quam artificium quod manu atque opere artificus exercetur. Multo enim est majus atque altius scire quod quisque faciat, quam ipsum illud efficere quod sciat; etenim artificium corporale, quasi serviens famulatur. Ratio vero quasi domina imperat et nisi manus secundum id quod ratio sancit efficiat, frustra fit. Quanto igitur praeclarior est scientia musicae in cognitione rationis, quam in opere efficiendi atque actu tantum scilicit quantum corpus menti superatur! Quod scilicet rationis expers servitio degit, illa vero imperat, atque ad rectum deducit, quod nisi pareat ejus imperio, et expers rationis opus titubabit. Unde fit ut speculatio rationis operandi actu non egeat. Manum vero opera nulla sint, nisi ratione ducantur. Iam vero quanta sit gloria meritumque, rationis hic intelligi potest, quod caeteri (ut ita dicam) corporales artifices non est ex disciplina, sed ex ipsis potius instrumentis cepere vocabula. Nam citharoedus ex cithara vel tibicen ex tibia caeterique suorum instrumentorum vocabulis nuncupantur. Is vero est musicus qui, ratione perpensa, canendi scientiam, non servitio operis sed imperio speculationis assumit. Quod scilicet in aedificiorum bellorumque opera videmus et in contraria scilicet nuncupatione vocabuli. Eorum namque nominibus vel aedificia inscribuntur vel ducuntur triumphi, quorum imperio ac ratione instituta sunt, non quorum opera servitioque perfecta. Tria sunt igitur genera quae circa artem musicam versantur; usum genus est quod instrumentis agitur, aluid fingit carmina. tertium quod instrumentorum opus carmenque dejudicat. Sed illud quidam quod instrumentis positum est, ibique totam operam consumit, ut sunt citharoedi, quique organo caeterisque musicae instrumentis artificium probant, a musicae scientiae intellectu sejuncti sunt quoniam famulantur (ut dictum est) nec quidquam afferunt rationis sed sunt totius speculationis expertes. Secundum vero musicam agentium est genus poetarum, quod non potius speculatione ac ratione quam naturali quodam instinctu fertur ad carmen, atque idcirco hoc quoque genus a musica segregandum est.

Tertium est quod judicandi peritiam sumit ut rhythmos cantilenasque corumque carmen possit perpendere. Quod scilicet quando totum in ratione ac speculatione positum est, hoc proprie musicae deputabitur. Isque musicus est cui adest facultas secundum speculationem rationemve propositam ac musicae convenientem de modis ac rhythmis deque generibus cantilenarum ac de permixtioribus ac de omnibus de quibus posterius explicandum `est ac de poetarum carminibus judicandi; ad majus ejusque principium unitas est qua minus nihil est.

LATIN TEXT: DE MUSICA—PATR. CH. i. P. 1171—"Inde est enim quod infantes quoque cantilena dulcis oblectat."
ibid ut supra. "Quid quod cum aliquis cantilenam libentius auribus atque animo capit, ad illud etiam non sponte convertitur, ut motum quoque aliquem similem auditae cantilenae. Corpus effugiat et

quod omnino aliquod melos auditum sibi memor animus ipse decerpat." (p. 1171).

. . ."Ut nulla omnino sit aetas quae a cantilenae dulcis delectatione sejuncta sit." (p. 1168).

. . . "Vulgatum quippe est quam saepe iracundias cantilena represserit." (p. 1170).

. . . "cum diurnas in somno resolverent curas quibusdam cantilenas uterentur ut eis lenis et quietus sopor irreperet." (p. 1170 infra).

. . . "sic non sufficit cantilenis musicis delectari, nisi etiam quali inter se conjunctae sint vocum proportione discatur." (p. 1171, ch. i, infra)

P. 1171— ch. ii.—"Et prima quidem mundana est : secuna vero humana, tertia quae in quibusdam constituta est instrumentis ut in cithara vel in tibiis, caeterisque quae cantilenae famulantur."

NOTE II

S. THOMAS AQUINAS

(SUMMA QUEST : 91, ACT ii, P. 646, VOL. 4, SEC : SECUNDAE)

I answer that as it has been pointed out vocal praise is necessary that human affection may be called forth to God. And, therefore, whatever furthers this end is of use, and fitly adopted for divine praise. It is clear that the souls of men are diversely disposed according to the diversity of the melodies of the jubilations (sonorum) as is apparent from Aristotle (Politic lib. viii, Cap. 5, 6 et 7) and Boethius (in prologo musica, seu. lib 1, Cap. 1 a med.). And therefore it has been healthfully laid down that in the Divine Praises singing should be used, that weak souls might be urged to devotion.

Whence S Augustine says (Confess : lib x, Cap 33 a med) : "I bring forward with approval the custom of singing in Church, that through aural appeal a weak soul may be spurred on to affective piety." And in regard to himself he says (Confess : lib ix, Cap 6 in fine): "I wept listening to your hymns and canticles, quickly moved by the voices of your appealing Assembly" (Ecclesiae).

CHAPTER II

Classical Use and Significance of Jubilatio

Classical Use and Significance of Jubilatio

The classical use and significance of "jubilatio" corroborates the meaning and implication applied to it by ecclesiastical writers. Sextus Pompeius Festus, who probably lived in the second century A.D., abridged a celebrated grammatical work, *De Verborum Significatu*, of one Verrius Flaccus, who flourished in the time of Augustus. At the close of the eighth century, Paul the Deacon epitomised Festus's abridgement of the original work of Verrius Flaccus. From this epitome of Paul* there is the following definition or explanation: "Jubilare est rustica voce inclamare"—"To jubilate is to make a joyful call like a peasant."

Lucius Apuleius about A.D. 125 in one of the episodes of his *Metamorphoses* describes a painful adventure. It is worth quoting at length, if only to show the antiquity of the peasant's outlook in his suspicion of strangers. †"Villae vero, quam tunc forte praeteribamus, coloni, multitudinem nostram latrones rati, satis agentes rerum suarum eximieque trepidi, canes rabidos et immanes et quibusvis lupis et ursis saeviores, quos ad tutelae praesidia curiosa fuerant alumnati, "jubilationibus solitis et cujuscemodi vocibus" nobis inhortantur qui praeter genuinam ferocitatem tumultu suorum exasperati contra nos ruunt, et, sine ullo dilectu jumenta simul et homines laeserant, diuque grassati plerosque prosternant."

Translation: "But the peasants of the village which we were then by chance passing by, exceedingly alarmed at our numbers, convinced we were robbers, with an eye to their property, set on us wild and savage dogs fiercer even than some wolves or bears, which they had carefully trained to protect their safety, they urged the dogs on us "with their accustomed calls and cries of this kind," who exasperated beyond their usual ferocity by the confusion caused by their own masters, sprang at us, and we having

---

* Festus: *De verborum significatu*. Cum Pauli Epitoma ed. W. M. Lindsay.
† Apuleius Met. 8, p. 17, Loeb. Edit.

been surrounded on all sides the dogs rushed in hither and thither and without more ado they bit beasts as well as men, and having violently attacked us, at length they pulled many down to the ground."

Then there is a very interesting explanation of jubilare in Marcus Terentius Varro, the contemporary of Cicero who contrasts jubilare with quiritare in his work *De Lingua Latina* (VI, 68): "Vicina horum quiritare, jubilare. Quiritare dicitur is qui Quiritum fidem clamans implorat . . . ut quiritare urbanorum, sic jubilare rusticorum, itaque nos imitans Aprissius ait: 'Io bucco! Quis me jubilat? Vicinus tuus antiquus?'"

Translation: "Allied to these words, just mentioned are 'Quiritare', 'to call plaintively', and 'jubilare', 'to call joyfully'. A man who is much in need of the protection of the Quirites is said to give the plaintive call of the Quirites, thus quiritare is a town and jubilare a country cry; therefore imitating us Apprissius says: 'Hullo fat-face, who gives me the joy call?' 'Your old neighbour.'"

S. Hilary (d. 368) has an interesting note on Psalm 65 showing he was well aware of the popular use of the word "jubilus", and how the force and meaning of the term persisted in his time, still bearing its classical significance. Commenting on Psalm 65 "Jubilate Deo", he writes: "What is commonly a 'jubilus'. According to the force of the Greek word, it is a military call—in the Latin *Codices* we read thus: 'Sing a jubilation to God all the earth.' And according to the custom of our language, we name the call of the peasant and agricultural worker a 'jubilus', when in solitary places, either answering or calling, the jubilation (sonus) of the voice is heard through the emphasis of the long drawn out and expressive rendering. In the Greek books, which are nearest to the Hebrew, the same significance is not apparent. For they have it in this fashion: 'alalaxate tō Theo pasa he gē'—they use alalagmus where Latin has 'jubilus'. It indicates the call of the advancing army, either in the charge of defeating the enemy, or by the call of witness following on the exultant victory. A cry of exultation differs from a jubilus, but for want of a better term in translation it can pass as 'jubilus'."

S. Cyril of Alexandria commenting on Psalm 94, "Venite", states: "A jubilation is a call of triumph which is sent forth to a wounded foe and a conquered enemy—come therefore and sing a jubilation to our Saviour and Redeemer."* In these quotations classical usage is carried forward, and in a sense, consolidated in

---

* Psalm 94 Comment (Migne Patr. p. 1239): "Jubilate vox quaedam est triumphalis, quae emittitur hostibus caesis et inimicis eversis. Venite igitur, jubilemus Salvatori ac Redemptori."

ecclesiastical custom and becomes part of a Catholic tradition. It therefore forms contact with the great classical tradition of drama and its sources, the original dance and song of the people surrounding the fertility rites and worship of remote ages. Song and dance became the medium of expression and where words failed and still greater emphasis was required to describe the emotional experience, "jubilatio" was the term used for this particular condition.

From a study of the context, it is clear that a mere shout is not implied by these words, but a distinctive call, furthermore, the two words in the last passage from Varro are contrasted, a plaintive and a joyful call. S. Augustine's use of "jubilare" is not therefore solely ecclesiastical because the classical writers, already quoted, refer to jubilare in the same sense and with the same significance as S. Augustine and others use the term. It is the age-long practice of the folk to make use of distinctive calls, or more correctly, beautiful musical curves and cadences to draw the attention of beasts as well as human beings. Witness the street cries of old London and elsewhere, still not entirely extinct. The urge here is to sell things and therefore attract attention. Sheep and cattle need the guiding call. It is hardly necessary to quote the Gospels to justify this statement. With the evidence before us Catholic theologians turned the practice into other channels, but as classical usage shows, they did not create a new musical system, for the joy of life as expressed by the "jubilation" was in the soul of man and more especially in the souls of those whose life lay nearest to mother earth, the peasant workers. There is little question what use the musicians of a much later age made of the street cries, for instance, Orlando Gibbons, Handel* and others.

It is possible in these days to trace the origin of the melodies for composed songs and for instruments, to this particular folk source. The custom is not extinct; an old cockle seller passes my door and challenged me to reproduce his call, a lovely curving jubilation. I did not accept his challenge. Lavender sellers will still jubilate in districts where fastidious "residents" do not further disfigure the entrances to their homes by placing on already un-attractive iron gates unimaginative notices—"No street cries."†

---

* *Notes on London Street Cries*, *J.F.S.S.* No. 22, 1919.

† It is important to refer to Dr. O. M. Sandvik's paper on Norwegian Folk Music which appears in the *Journal of the E.F.D.S.S.*, Vol. ii, International Festival No. 1935. Studying Dr. Sandvik's statement there seems little doubt in his mind as to the source of Gregorian melodies and also the meaning of "flowering grace notes", as he calls them, of the folksinger. It is the perpetuation of the " jubilatio " under circumstances similar to the primitive ages. Dr. Sandvik mentions the cattle call of the Irish peasant in this connection.

NOTE I

Some years ago after giving a lecture which covered the ground of this present treatise before the Summer School of the English Folk Dance Society, I received a very interesting comment from the late Mr. H. W. Nevinson. After the lecture Mr. Nevinson said to me : "I do not know if you are aware that this custom which you described as singing on 'vowel sounds' is still to be found among the Greeks and Turks." I wrote to Mr. Nevinson shortly before his death and received the following reply :

"We both remember your admirable lecture on Ecclesiastical Music very well. I am not musician enough to write with authority but, if you wish, you might certainly quote me as observing the same distinctive quality in modern Greek, Turkish, and even N. Indian song. A long drawn out quavering note is common to them all; and I believe the note is always a 'vowel sound'. In fact I am sure of it. I do not know where this strange quavering song originated, but it certainly pervades all the Middle East. I cannot speak for China."

It is quite unnecessary to dwell on the late Mr. Nevinson's wide experience of the lives of the people in many lands; those of us who knew him and listened to his lectures quickly realised that he was the very person to notice features of this description in quite remote corners of the world. Others might pass over such customs without seeing their underlying significance, but not Mr. Nevinson. As I have pointed out, these vocal customs represent the "soul" of the people and have great cultural importance, besides being of historical value when tracing the history of musical development.

I feel this letter is a valuable piece of confirmatory evidence. However, the chant may have "settled" in the Gregorian period, or shown very distinct advancement in technical art in the ninth century, yet the source is obvious, the folk were always there with their own unselfconscious song, in artistic expression perhaps more satisfactory than the voices of the cantors at the lectern.

CHAPTER III

Conscious and Unconscious Rhythm

CHAPTER III

Conscious and Unconscious Rhythm

The Mystical Significance of the Jubilatio

RHYTHM may be described as that quality which gives meaning and expression to the higher or spiritual side of life. There is, of course, a more formal or technical description, but, just as Christian theology cannot explain the nature of God, neither can rhythm, nor any other term, explain the action of the soul in its contact and operation with the circumstances of its physical environment. Dealing with the question of language alone, we have here the central means both of self and mutual expression, but language is not the medium for fulfilling purely material needs; language is the medium whereby mankind can approach his own being and realise it is formed of body, soul and spirit. S. Augustine noticed with wonder and interest how the peasant sang with his whole soul, from sheer joy, and with the desire to be at one with the natural order of life. Christians at prayer follow the same method, but the result became transposed or transfigured into the supernatural order or condition. It was not accidental that the peasant sang using only the vowel sound to express his emotion, there is a distinct spiritual significance unconscious in the peasant, attached to this practice.

Dr. Rudolph Steiner writes : "You will feel if you pronounce a vowel sound, that you are giving expression to something coming from the inmost depths of our own being. Every vowel . . . is bound up with an experience of the soul."* It is well to quote the words of a modern philosopher because, whatever the age or period, rhythm remains the underlying or sacramental quality which gives life and meaning to every form of art. It is a straightforward matter to follow up the theme throughout the centuries,

---

* *Eurhythmy as Visible Speech*, p. 12, ff.

mystics and saints found more than joy when the method of the folk singer was transferred to Christian prayer and worship and raised to a higher plane.

Jubilatio became part of the mystical phenomena relating to the prayer of quiet. The fourteenth century English mystic, Richard Rolle of Hampole, calls this state "Canor or Song". He writes in *The Fire of Love* :* "Because he has continually given himself to constant devotion for God when Christ wills He shall receive—not of his own need but of Christ's goodness—a Holy sound sent from Heaven, and thought and meditation shall be changed into song, and the mind shall bide in marvellous melody . . . soothly it happens to such a lover what I have not found in the writings of the Doctors; that is, this song shall swell up in his mouth, and he shall sing his prayers with a ghostly symphony; and he shall be slow with his tongue, because of the great plenty of inward joy tarrying in song and singular sound, so that that he was wont to say in an hour scarcely he may fulfil in a day. Whilst he receives it soothly he shall sit alone, not singing with others nor reading psalms." This experience is not absolutely singular, but Rolle seems to possess it in a marked degree and he also has the capacity for self-analysis and literary self-expression.

The same condition occurs in the life of S. Teresa,† the jubilation is a state of ecstasy or intoxication, the unconscious art of the peasant folk singer has become the conscious prayer of the mystic because it emanates from the same subconscious source. The folk method has been grafted on to the Divine Office, it is soil where the growth of the soul expands, it has become the foundation for infinite spiritual development. We shall examine and see in the course of this essay how the Western Church responded in detail to the suggestion of S. Augustine and others. In the spheres of music and drama alone the results have been nearly incalculable. Looking at the question from a slightly different angle, we may say the jubilatio is the movement of sound vibration through a human form, Rudolph Steiner writes§ : "The human form stands before us—that most wonderful of earthly forms—the human form stands before us and we ask the Divine Spiritual powers which have existed from the beginning : How then did you create man? Did you create him in some such way as the spoken word is created when we speak? How did you create man? What really took place when you created man? And if we were to receive an

---

* *Fire of Love*, p. 137, ff., edit. J. M. M. Comper.
† *The Graces of Interior Prayer*, R. P. Poulain, Jubil. xiv, 23 bis.
§ *Eurhythmy*, p. 15.

answer to our question from out of universal space it would be some such answer as this : All around us there is movement, form, constantly and of infinite variety . . . all possibilities of form in movement receive from out of the Universe, every possibility of movement that we out of the nature of our being are able to conceive and to bring into connection with the human organisation."

S. Thomas Aquinas has also a very interesting passage on how human contacts are preserved with Divine Reality. Steiner, too, seems to echo these views of S. Thomas on movement and its significance in relation to physical life.

Speaking of prayer and contemplation as methods of inducement to arrive at that rhythm which tends towards perfection of motion, S. Thomas writes :* "A spiritual operation in which contemplation essentially consists is called motion in that movement is characteristic of a perfect act as Aristotle says. Because we proceed through the things of sense into the knowledge of things spiritual, thence it is that even spiritual operations are indeed described as motion and according to the appearance of the diverse movements their difference is assigned. Now in the movement of bodies the more perfect and the primary ones have position (locales). And therefore the principal spiritual operations are described under this appearance (of position). They are three different movements, for instance, circular whereby anything is moved uniformly round its centre; next straight (rectus) according to which a thing proceeds from one to another; and the third oblique (a serpentine movement) which is made up of both circular and straight."

S. Thomas applies this description strictly speaking to the movement of the angelic beings, there arises a "difformity" between perfect motion and its counterpart in the rhythm of human life, but relationship is not excluded in spite of this difformity because the psychological basis of both is identical, the combination in this life of spiritual and physical vibrations finding expresssion in jubilatio or even where all forms of utterance fail, expression through movement in the dance.†

Now the statement quoted from S. Thomas is not only wonderful choreography, it is also primeval magic. How did the human

---

* *Summa Secunda Secundae Quest* : clxxx, Art vi. vid. Appendix Latine.

† Gehbert : *De Cantu et Musica Sacra*, p. 299 quotes S. Augustine *De Musica* : "Ergo scientiam modulandi jam probabile est esse scientiam bene movendi," which might be paraphrased to mean "If you know the rhythm of singing you probably understand the rhythm of the dance." See note at end of this chapter for the entire quotation from S. Augustine "De Musica".

race express its subconscious impulses, make contact with the unseen, induce and promote the divine life within and without, but through the movements of the dance circularis, rectus, obliquus, it is the divine rhythm blending spiritual vibrations with physical which has been found to give the greatest joy and satisfaction and which reveal the spiritual nature of man and his ultimate end.

To return once more to vowel sounds and the use of speech, Steiner says :* "A vowel sound is always the expression of some aspect of the feeling life of the soul . . . every vowel sound does in its essence express some shade of the feeling life of the soul; and this feeling only has to unite itself with thought, with the head system, in order to pass over into speech. What I have said about the vowel sounds of speech can be applied equally to the tones of music. The various sounds of speech, the use of idiom, the construction of phrases and sentences—all these things are the expression of the feeling life of the soul. In singing also the soul life expresses itself through tone." Steiner is here illustrating the qualitative character of rhythm and appealing for the realisation of its necessity before any real artistic self-expression can be attained. It is a clear instance of spiritual or soul value as the inspiration for effective action in the sphere of our material environment. As we have seen, it is what S. Augustine and S. Thomas Aquinas understood only too well, the same divine treasury supplying to mankind things new and old. So far we have dealt almost exclusively with unconscious musical rhythm, this has been essential in order to show the source and inspiration of conscious bodily action.†

I am well aware that the psychological basis of the foregoing statement may well be challenged, it is not the psychology of the materialist. Modern psychology may have its own explanation for the phenomena surrounding the life of primitive man, but whether this explanation is a fair analysis of the mind of humanity is another matter. The study of folklore has opened up a very wide field for research, but is it possible for us to understand the mentality of our remote ancestors when we today want to eliminate

---

* Steiner: *Eurhythmy as Visible Song*, p. 29.

† Vid. *A Search in Secret India*. Paul Brunton, who writes p. 243: "The writings I am studying say that sound is the force which called the universe into being. . . . A current of sound was the first activity of the Supreme Being at the beginning of creation."

We do not mean any material sound but a spiritual one. The force which appears as sound on our material plane is only the reflection of that subtler force whose workings evolved the universe. A sound carries the influence of the region whence it emanates.

what was their chief interest, the soul? Their whole economy was identified with the mystery of life; growth and life were not merely physical processes but allied to mankind in his yearning to know and experience the life-giving forces surrounding him, it was his conception of God, whose power he induced and on whom he ultimately depended. This attitude represented a settled faith and therefore a concentrated and determined mental and spiritual effort. If the mind of the modernist does not enter into this experience, how can he ultimately judge or analyse the mental environment of an age utterly remote from his own? There is no illusion in the matter; with a strong bias in a materialistic direction, how can we appreciate a psychological condition completely alien to our modern scientific background?

The whole philosophy of art has arisen from the worship of fertility with the customs and ceremonial attached to it. Speech and song, form, colour, movement, are imbedded in the lives of the people and their worship. Its very spontaneity shows its foundation in the subconscious, its manifestation we call inspiration or rhythm, the expression of the human imagination which surely can only be described as a spiritual faculty.* Perhaps it is through the imaginaton that we arrive at the rhythmical core of art. Rhythm and imagination may be independent, but the former will justify the vision of the latter because it creates the atmosphere where the imagination can best perform its real functions. Hume† called imagination a magical faculty, and Professor Fawcett refers to it as the "Plastic psychical stuff in which all human activities (including those artificially isolated as faculties) have their being." The imagination then is the power which brings reality into the ideal. The imagination, as a rhythmical movement, cannot for long linger in the realm of the abstract but must seek for concrete self-expression, for some self-satisfying medium whereby the same imaginative impulse has both an outlet and completion. Now if this conception is pivotal in human relations, we might then urge that it is "The Power" of which Wordsworth writes :

---

* See Professor Marett's *Psychology and Folklore,* p. 14, ff., for a study of "Transformism" and its relation to the matter referred to in the text, also Professor George Thomson's two works, *Marxism and Poetry* and *Aeschylus and Athens.* Although I disagree with Professor Thomson on the theory of "illusion" in reference to the question of fertility worship, yet I am extremely grateful for the two books mentioned above, the study of both seems essential to the subject in hand.

† See F. D. Fawcett: *The World as Imagination.* p. 135, ff.

> I have felt
> A Presence that disturbs me with the joy
> Of elevated thoughts; a sense sublime
> Of something far more deeply interfused
> Whose dwelling is the light of setting suns
> And the round ocean and the living air
> And the blue sky and in the mind of man
> A motion, and a spirit, that impels
> All thinking things, all objects of all thought,
> And rolls through all things.

These poetic words reveal not only a sense of rhythm but are an analysis of the source of the human imagination, the centre from which all art is generated, above all it is the beginning of that aesthetic experience which culminates in what we call the works of art. As we have suggested, examples are abundant. The divinity that is enshrined in the work of the men of the palaeolithic age is a well-known instance. Here the food of man is identified with the God man seeks to worship. But only the supreme imaginative effort could enable mankind to see beyond the physical need resulting from hunger to a divine union of both physical and spiritual forces. The palaeolithic age did not produce pictures, it reached forth to the divine through the power of vision centred in the imagination, it saw beyond the material into the spiritual. Hence its art is not pictorial but symbolic, enshrining a rite, a mystery of initiation, whereby the initiated found their unity with, and their power over, their God.

We find the same spirit throughout the ages, the really great and enduring things that any group or community have performed are the result of the rhythm of the imagination and the culture or civilisation which has arisen has been fundamentally religious, its roots are to be found primarily in a religious or spiritual impulse the result of emotional urge. The indications of the Catholic culture are palpable in the rhythm of form, colour, sound and movement, the buildings of the Middle Ages enshrined a worship founded in an unselfconscious expression of a rhythm of life which permeated the whole of society. Art at this period represented a unified achievement beyond the imagination of our present day efforts. We cannot hop back into the past, but at least we can appreciate and cultivate the under-lying principle of all culture, the rhythm of the imagination.*

---

* For a lucid and masterly account of the technique of formal rhythm, see *Grammar of Plainsong*. Stanbrook, Pt. ii, *Theory of Rhythm*. Also *Plainchant,* Dom Gatard. Gregorian Chironomy, Plate iv, p. 48.

NOTE

THE problem, when did the human race become melodically conscious must surely be largely a conjectural matter and intricate to solve. It has been urged that mankind's sense of rhythm arose through the use of tools, especially the vibrating blows of the hammer. There may be a certain tempo, a rhythm in the beat of a hammer when wielded with precision, but surely melody arose through human emotion which obviously applies to every type of Folksong. To extend this notion one might ask why do the birds sing? If we want to know how mankind became musically articulate, may he not have listened to the birds and followed the same vocal impulse? I submit that this conjecture is as valid as any other suggestion of a similar nature. I will now refer to the Journal of the International Folk Music Council (Vol. vi, 1954) to an article on the Music of Norwegian Lapland by Ragnwald Graff. The opening sentences of this article are most significant—"The Northern part of Scandinavia is partly inhabited by a remarkable race of people, who both anthropologically and in their language stand quite apart from the surrounding populations. Their origin is not known, but traces of the Lappish stone age culture dating back some 2000 years B.C. have been found, and they are mentioned in our old Viking sagas." This learned author continues (p. 29): "Returning from one of my voyages in Norwegian Lapland I sang a juoik (folksong) to one of my Norwegian friends from Tromso. It was a song without words which is associated with one of our Arctic birds 'havella' (Clangula hyemalis). On hearing the tune, he was at once able to tell which bird was described by the song. The Lapp who sang this song for me, said jestingly that the bird itself had composed it."

I wish I had space to quote the whole of this article but the short extract I have already given serves to show a very deep-rooted tradition amongst a nation whose Folklore dates back to a very remote past and furthermore does not seem to have undergone any very fundamental change in the passage of time. The statement certainly seems to justify the suggestion that melodic self-expression may have arisen from the song of the birds.

INITIUM CAP. II, S. AUGUSTINE DE MUSICA, (PATR: P. 1083).
"What is Music? What does 'Modulating' mean?"

M. Now it matters very little to us troubling about the name; we will enquire presently if it is well, how to make a careful enquiry, because it is characteristic of this study to find out what has force and reason.

34

D. We may profitably enquire for this is a self-contained matter;
I want to know more about it.

M. Therefore define music.

D. I dare not.

M. At the same time can you prove my definition?

D. I will make an attempt, if you will tell me.

M. Music is the knowledge of good rhythm, is this not your view?

D. Perhaps it might be, if it could be clear to me what rhythm
really is.

M. Is not this word described as "to modulate" something you
have never heard anywhere except where it applies to singing
and dancing?

D. So it is indeed : but because I see rhythm in the manner aforesaid, a method observed in good performance and applied to
singing and dancing, and although they give pleasure, yet they
may be most undesirable, I want to know very clearly what
rhythm is in itself whereby possessing the word a definition
is decided with understanding for nothing is to be learnt by
such methods merely because it is known to singers and actors.

M. What you said above in regard to method applies to everything except music and yet in music rhythm is evoked not to
stir feeling; unless you are ignorant of what is properly called
the diction of an orator.

D. I am not ignorant, but what's your point?

M. Well, take any boy you like, however simple and un-
sophisticated, when in response to a question he replies with
a single word, do you admit that he says anything?

D. Yes, I admit it.

M. Therefore that boy is an orator?

D. No!

M. Not by the diction he has used; therefore what you first of
all felt are many undesirable features in singing and dancing,
whereby if we accept the term rhythm godly learning itself is
degraded; an observation on your part altogether indefensible.
Therefore, let us discuss first of all what rhythm is, then
what it is to modulate with effect for it is not inappropriate
to add to the definition. Finally what knowledge has established ought not to be despised, for on these three points,
unless I am mistaken perfect definition is to be found.

D. I quite agree.

M. Let us acknowledge therefore that rhythm is named from a
particular method, does it not appear to you to be matter for
hesitation lest the method be exaggerated or not, to fulfil its

purpose, except in the matters which take place in any movement? Or if there is no movement can we fear lest something
may happen contrary to the method?

D. By no means.

M. Therefore, "rhythm" is not incongruously called "a certain
neatness (peritia) in movement" for surely it comes about that
something may move attractively. For we cannot urge that
anything moves attractively if it does not keep to the form
and method.

D. Indeed we cannot; but it will be necessary again to realise
that this rhythm is in everything neatly acomplished. I see
nothing well done without rhythmical movement.

M. What happens if all these things come about through music
although the term rhythm applied to instruments of any kind
may be rather commonplace but not without effect? For I
believe on the one hand a thing may seem to you to be turned
out in wood or metal or any material you like, but on the
other hand it may be the impulse of the craftsman himself,
when these things are fashioned.

D. I agree they differ considerably.

M. Does not the impulse arise from its own volition and not
from the necessity to make something?

D. It is obvious.

M. But why? If the hands might not move for any other reason
save in a comely and beautiful manner we might urge that
he does nothing less when he dances.

D. So it seems.

M. When therefore do you consider any circumstance to be outstanding and as it were to dominate the situation? When it
arises spontaneously or when it is sought for some other motive?

D. When it is spontaneous; does anyone deny it?

M. Repeat now what we said above about rhythm; we had
postulated it as a certain neatness of movement, and look
where the foundation is firm there the name should be; in
that movement which is spontaneous being personally acquired
for its own sake and by this means finds satisfaction, or who,
in a certain manner, is absorbed in it; for all things as it were
perform service which are not personal but seek some other
good.

D. For example, that which is sought for its own sake.
Therefore, the science of rhythm is probably knowing how to
move with graceful precision, in such a manner that the inward

impulse thus acquired and through that experience finds true satisfaction.

D. You are probably correct.

CHAPTER IV

Historical Development

Historical Development

As we have already seen the text of the Catholic Liturgy was founded on the Holy Scriptures, the Psalter being the basis for the chant. S. Gregory introduced certain changes in the accustomed method of singing, but what these alterations were, it is difficult to write definitely. John the Deacon (*circa* 870) wrote about the great Pope's treatment of the Gelasian Sacramentary: "Multa subtrahens, pauca convertens, non-nulla vero superadiciens." (Taking away much, changing a few things, adding something.) Unfortunately this statement was made some centuries after S. Gregory's time but S. Gregory's influence in this direction had become so general that it is difficult not to accept this tradition as accurate, so long as undue emphasis is not placed upon it, for instance, the notion sometimes advanced that S. Gregory "invented" the chant. He may certainly have shortened the "melisma" or jubilations, the folk, once started on a theme, like to continue (ad libitum) as Cassiodorus tells us was his actual experience amongst Christian congregations in his day. The Pope may have felt that a certain term had to be placed on this prevalent custom, hence the description of his reforms by John the Deacon.* Again, John the Deacon's statement may also refer to the text of the liturgy as well as the music where, too, the Apostolic See felt alterations were necessary.† There is also the well-established tradition that S. Gregory founded the Roman Schola or School of Singers, their influence was felt throughout the churches and monasteries of the

---

* See *Plainchant*, by the late Dom Gatard, O.S.B., who wrote as follows (p. 34, ff): "Dom Germain Morin seems to be on the right track when he compares the great Pope's work on the Antiphoner to that which is attributed to him by John the Deacon on the Gelasian Sacramentary. The Ambrosian Chant, as given in the oldest MSS, is held by many to be precisely the form which Gregory simplified." See also *English Folksongs—Some Conclusions,*" Ch. V, C. J. Sharp.

† Vid. Rule of S. Benedict, Ch. XII. ". . . Canticum unumquodaue die suo exprohpetis sicut psallit Ecclesia Romana, dicatur. Vid. p. 42. Council of Cloveshoo.

West for centuries. We know pilgrims from this and other countries to Rome through the seventh and eighth centuries were greatly impressed by the chanting of the Gregorian Schola.*

All this rather points to the chant becoming a distinct system, the vocal customs of the folk gradually being interpreted in the terms of art formulae.

*   *   *   *

By the ninth century we are on more certain ground. Liturgical MSS, containing a form of musical notation, have been preserved and it is to these MSS in recent years recourse has been made to discover the true nature of the chant. The earliest form of this notation is fascinating to the student of folksong, because it shows how entirely traditional the form and pitch of the melody was, since there is no indication from the notation what the form and pitch could have been. The very name of this notation, "chironomic", indicates the striving of the master of the Schola to obtain continuity of melody and execution.† The system may have arisen from the guiding hand of the precentor, that is, following the upward and downward stroke, not of course in strict metrical beat in the modern sense, but to feel the range and rhythm of the melody. Voice and hand, or voice and gesture, if you will, working together. This early notation may therefore be little more than the acute accent (ˊ) and the grave accent (ˋ)—the acute accent indicating the upward curve and the grave accent the cadence. It is surprising that there is no definite evidence for this distinctive type of notation till the ninth century because, given a knowledge of the form of the melody, the notation, for instance, which appears in the MS of S. Gall, shows a certain advanced stage in notational development. This matter has been fully dealt with by Dom

---

* All due emphasis too should be placed on the Roman musical missions, James the precentor at York and also Petrus and Romanus. See Wagner: *Hist. of Plainchant*, pp. 202, 220.

† See Stanbrook: *Georgian Music*, p. 14. "We know how intimate is the connection between voice and hand, both are ruled simultaneously by movement of the soul: 'Gestus et ipse voci consentit et animo cum eo simul paret'. (Quintilian Inst. Orat. xi, 3). So true is this and so natural, that the very accents are merely graphic representations of those gestures, and take their form from the motion of the speaker's hand." Also (p. 17) a quotation from Guido Aretinus, "De ignoto cantu". "Mirabiles autem cantores et cantorum discipuli, etiamsi per centum annos cantent nunquam per se sine magistro unam vel saltem parvulam antiphonam cantabunt. . . ." Compare, too, Cath: Euc. Vol. X, art. Neum. Professor Bewerunge sums up his examination in the following words: "It is clear, then, that at no time could the melody be read absolutely from the neumatic notation. Rather this served merely as an aid to memory. Nor did the choir sing from the notation. The MS was only for the choir-master or at most for the solo singer."

Gregory Sunol,* who rather supports the idea that an examination of fragments older than ninth century MSS suggests greater antiquity for the chironomic notation.

Dom Sunol further supports this contention by reference to the Council of Cloveshoo† (Decr. xiii) : "In the Office of Baptism, in the celebration of Masses, they shall follow the manner of singing according to the copy written for example which we have from the Roman Church." This Council met in the middle of the eighth century (*circa* 747) so it is possible that some sort of marks bearing notation value may be appearing in the codices by the eighth century, but this theory is largely based on the assumption that we know what was written, "juxta exemplar", mentioned in the decree of the Council of Cloveshoo, whereas we have to be very sure we are not interpreting an eighth century document in the light of very much later musical traditions. Even if some form of notation was referred to, the notation, however described, would have been no melodic guide to the cantor.§ It might surely be equally well urged that this decree refers to the text of the liturgy which, according to the twelfth decree of the same council, was not to be corrupted or interfered with, (corrumpant vel confundant). And again in the fifteenth decree : "Nothing that common use does not allow shall they presume to sing or read, but only what has come down from the authority of Holy Scripture and what the custom of the Roman Church permits shall they sing or read." If it is not too obvious, twelfth century notation and instructions, in regard to the chant, cannot enter into the discussion at this juncture, therefore, whatever the "exemplar" referred to, in the strictly musical sense, would not have been of very great assistance, but when dealing with the actual wording of the Rites of Baptism and the Mass, might have a very different effect. Dom Sunol even goes further and adds : "It was not merely an oral tradition that S. Augustine of Canterbury took to England . . . but a "codex" which contained melodies (in cantilenae modo) and which was sent from Rome by order of Pope Gregory the Great." But what a surprising assumption ! We certainly have a codex for which there is evidence to support the tradition that it was

---

* *Introduction à la Paléographie musicale grégorienne* 1935. *Introduccio a la Paleografia Musical Gregoriana* per Dom Gregori Ma. Sunyol, O.S.B. Abadia de Monserrat, MCMXXV.

† Latin text of the decrees vid. appendix.

‡ Wagner : *Hist. of Plainchant*, p. 34, states that " They (the cantors) had the text on a leaf before them ; they themselves added the melody to it." The whole passage, with the notes, requires careful study but this writer certainly seems to favour the position adopted in the text.

actually sent to Canterbury by S. Gregory, the famous Canterbury Gospels (Evangelica Cantuariensia),* but there is no sign of any musical notation in this MS. It may be worth while to notice that this MS probably was used through the ages for the ceremonial singing of the Gospel at the Liturgy.   Dom Sunol continues :† "It would be difficult to imagine how these missionary monks (S. Augustine's companions) setting out from Rome for England could have taken to those distant regions the whole musical treasure of the Roman Church, if they had been without any written music and had trusted to their memory alone." Surely this is purely a modern supposition? Does Dom Sunol here mean to deny what he has previously stated (p. 22) that "These neums . . . indicate merely the number of the notes and a relative undetermined pitch not their final tonal value."

Whatever this real or supposed Gregorian Codex may have contained by way of neums or signs does not mean it possessed formal melodies, because even the "developed" ninth century notation never suggests exactly the form and theme of the melody so if actual notation existed in the time of S. Augustine of Canterbury his monastic followers would still have been obliged to retain the melodies in their memories. In days when books were scarce and printing non-existent, when the capacity to read, write and cipher was not considered the beginning and ending of all culture, the human memory was vastly enhanced. The monks knew the psalter by heart : S. Benedict provides for this (vid. Reg. Ch. 48), so it is not surprising to find words and music "in memoria" yet still preserving an accurate tradition. It is hardly necessary to point out how well known this accuracy is to the folksong collector. Unlettered folk will sing song after song, words and melody quite distinct in each case, without hesitation entirely from memory.§

---

* Library of Corpus Christi College, Cambridge, MS 286.   Evangelica Cantuariensia assigned to the sixth century by Tischendorf.   Probably Italian showing marked affinity to the Codex Amiatinus. H. J. White does not agree with the tradition in regard to its source but the late Dom John Chapman considers that the MS is old enough to be what it is claimed to be. Personally, I favour Abbot Chapman's opinion in the matter of the date of this MS, which also contains two very interesting illuminations deserving careful examination from the standpoint of primitive ceremonial. (Vid. Catalogue MSS James C.C.C. Libr.)

† Through the kindness of the Father Abbot of Prinknash I have had access to the original Catalan version of Dom Sunol's work, and to the French translation containing an introduction by the late Dom Mocquereau, also to a most useful English translation in typescript. It is from the latter that I am quoting (p. 25).   I am sorry to have to join issue with some of Dom Sunol's conclusions. His work shows very considerable research, sound scholarship, and great knowledge of the chant.

§ Vid. C. J. Sharp: *English Folksongs*, p. 107.

Granted, variations appear in the words and music of the folk-songs, but these changes are not so much lapses of memory as the impact of fresh experience and altered conditions of life.

*   *   *   *

Returning once more to the question of the exact significance of the decree of the Council of Cloveshoo; it is well to stress the necessity for eliminating from our minds twentieth century environment with all that term implies, and not thrust back on the seventh or any other century a musical atmosphere not in the least consonant with the feeling and outlook of those times. As I have already suggested, the above statement of the Council of Cloveshoo might refer to the textual format of the Mass and Office, and since S. Gregory made several alterations in the text of the Sacramentary and the Liber Antiphonarius, this canon might be dealing with the wording of a text which the melodies were to emphasise and express. However, Dom Sunol* makes it quite clear that it was necessary to learn the whole of the Liturgy by heart so as to be able to tackle the notation however meagre or full its content might be. It is interesting reading how Dom Sunol works out the possible means and methods used by the primitive cantors when guided with or without chironomic notation, but he does not even refer to the obvious presence of the natural song of the people all over the world, a living form of music in which the said cantors must have shared from their earliest years to manhood.

Dom Sunol† would like to find the source of the notation of the MS of S. Gall at Rome and Italy. But from what source do we look for the foundation of the Abbey of S. Gall but to Ireland, the home of cultural security during the dark and difficult periods of barbarian invasion? May we not therefore suggest that the rise of a distinct technique or notation as applied to the chant arose from the homophonic (bardic) methods of the Irish harpists? The whole question of the source and evolution of Irish and Welsh homophonic music is dealt with in a learned article by Peter Crossley-Holland in *"Music and Letters."*§ Although this article does not deal directly with the source of the plainchant notation, and no definite theory is advanced, yet after studying its content nobody would want to draw too drastic conclusions in relation to the exact origin of the notation.

---

* op. cit. English translation, p. 31.

† op. cit. English translation, pp. 77–78.

§ April, 1942, Vol. 23, No. 2.

Remembering, too, the influence of Ireland on Catholic culture during the dark ages, such a suggestion is as capable of support from actual evidence as the rather settled suppositions of the sources of the plainchant notation which have been recently advanced.*

Dom Sunol explains the scheme of travel or "excursion" described on the map in his book † showing the spread of the chant. But the implication underlying the whole paragraph suggests musical ignorance on the part of the peoples concerned, whereas, whether they were Latin speaking or Barbarian, they were singing in their daily lives as S. Augustine, S. John Chrysostom and Cassiodorus tell us. Dom Sunol would look to Italy, and apparently to Italy alone, as the authentic and true source of the chant. "It is just that country (Italy) that was the cradle of plainsong, etc."§

But again, why should Italy be the cradle of the chant when singing was universal as patristic evidence shows? No one place can claim at any time a monopoly of that vocal expression which is common to the human race everywhere. Before printing was invented and before musical technique became more fully developed the contrast between ancient times and more modern situations is marked. The folk of those primitive ages did not require to be taught to sing as is the case with educated moderns, but their "soni" and "cantus" had to be allied to the liturgical texts.

*   *   *   *

In conclusion I must deal with a statement which S. Isidore makes on this very question of a written musical script. The period would be towards the end of the sixth and the beginning of the seventh century. He writes :

---

* After further correspondence with Mr. Crossley-Holland on the question of the possibility of Irish Bardic influence on the musical technique contained in the S. Gall MS, I fully admit that definite evidence is not forthcoming in support of such a theory. But I might refer to another branch of art where evidence does point in an Irish or Celtic direction —architecture, and more particularly decoration. Apparently Irishmen carried their decorative designs up the Rhine to settle in the monastery of S. Gall and elsewhere. If we accept unity in artistic expression, the studied technique found in Celtic stone pattern may possibly have appeared in another even more sensitive form of rhythm —vocal music. The idea stated may not therefore be entirely devoid of foundation. Vid. an important monograph: *Medieval Art in Sussex* by C. H. Blakiston (Sussex Church's Art Council Publication No. 2).

† P. 72.

§ English translation, Ch. IX, p. 108.

1. "Music is skill in inflection consisting in jubilation* and song: the term music is derived from the Muses which again is taken from the Greek mosthai, that is, by seeking what by this means the men of former days desired the emphasis of the songs and the inflection of the voice should be obtained.

2. "Therefore the jubilation, because it is a matter of sensitiveness, fades away into the past, but is impressed on the memory, thence by the poets of Jupiter the matter has been formed in the memory of the daughters of the Muses.

3. "For unless the jubilations (soni) are retained in human memory they perish because they cannot be written."†

In the first place, it is interesting to notice this reference to classical tradition on the part of S. Isidore, when seeking for an explanation for certain outstanding vocal customs and practices. But his conclusion seems perfectly definite and without qualification, the "soni" or jubilations, that is, the custom of singing without words and on vowel sounds, a tradition received in the first instance from the Muses, for permanence depends entirely on the human memory; in other words it is an oral and not a documentary tradition. Examining the whole passage, with its classical reference, it seems S. Isidore was as well aware as S. Augustine of the singing methods of the people.

If his words mean anything, we are surely obliged to admit the obvious conclusion that at all events in his day, the seventh century, there was no written musical script, in any form, of the melisma. At this time it was not necessary because jubilations were such a common practice. We can therefore conclude that, until much clearer evidence is forthcoming, the definite ninth century musical notation represents the first scientific attempt to describe in writing the melismatic chant. The slowness of the development perhaps shows that the memory of the precentor was paramount. He knew the melodies because he was living in the tradition, outside as well as within, the convent walls. The natural sense of tone had not been dulled or lost through the mechanical contrivances of modern life. The Divine Office only fired the human imagination still further and called forth the already innate feeling for the pure melody of the jubilations. None the less, we can indeed feel grateful to the scribes and musicians of the ninth

---

* The meaning of the Latin is clear "sono cantuque", that is, sono= singing on vowel sounds without words, and cantus=melody allied with words. See appendix for the quotation in Latin, also p. 4 for S. Augustine's term " in sonum jubilationis".

† *S. Isidore De Musica* 132, Ch. XV, Vol. 82, Etym. Libr. III (Patr. Lat.).

century for attempting a system of standardization because it preserved not only the melody but its method of execution, which means the true rendering and rhythm of the verbal and musical phrases.*

Hence after the attempt at spacing the neums, some scribe begins to utilise the line of the text as a starting point for the notation, having made use of one line, another follows, until a staff of four lines is found to be sufficient. Guy of Arezzo appears to have improved the system in the eleventh century, and from that time onwards the four line stave with signs and notation, now familiar to all who study the chant, gave the system permanent shape and definite meaning.† But system and order did not create the melodies, in fact, formal theory did not always correspond to the actual form of the melody. In the words of the writer of the article on plainchant in the *Catholic Encyclopaedia* : "It would, therefore, seem certain that the eight mode theory was, as a ready made system, imposed on the existing stock of plainchant melodies."

The ninth and tenth centuries were an age of great musical activity; monasteries, cathedrals, the Roman Schola, the Emperor Charlemagne, were all busily engaged in preserving the true tradition of the chant.

The work of the musicians of this period deserves careful study because there is evidence to show that in trying to fix the tradition, they did not neglect its source. They were most particular about the true meaning of the words of the liturgy and the musical phrases which were to enhance and emphasise their value and significance. The chant required the right balance, because perfect execution could only be achieved by pause and stress, the underlying principle of all verbal rhythm. We have now arrived at the stage of conscious rhythm, the former unselfconscious vocal and musical effort of the folksinger being treated as a technical system. Today we feel suspicious of such attempts, but the evidence surviving from the ninth century seems to show

---

* However, I feel this passage in the text requires a certain amount of qualification. Dom Sunol (op. cit. p. 67, ff.) draws attention to the effect on the chant resulting from an over emphasised technique as the neumatic notation developed to the detriment of the rhythm of the chant, causing the underlying spirit of the music to be forgotten. The student of folksong would certainly join with Dom Sunol when he adds this caution. In other words, do not attempt to fix musical rhythms which, from their very nature, cannot submit to formal fixity.

† Dom Sunol (op. cit. supra) points out that the evolution of the neum continued till the fourteenth century, but Germany apparently preserved the traditional chironomic forms for a longer period.

that the musicians of those days, steeped in a living tradition of song, understood very well the exact nature of the work in which they were engaged. They have left on record their attempts at standardization for the judgment and criticism of a later age.

NOTE

(This note deals with the rise of notation)

SINCE writing this chapter, I have been given further opportunities for investigation. Through the kindness of the department of Egyptology at Cambridge I have examined the facsimile copy of the Oxyrhynchus Papyri No. 1785, p. 21, part xv. This fragment is the result of the discoveries of Grenfell and Hunt and published in 1922. It represents a very ancient doxology and apparently contains musical signs or directives. The commentator makes the following observations. "Above each line of the text the corresponding vocal notes have been added in a more cursive lettering, whether by the same hand or another is not easy to determine. The character of both scripts appears to point to a date in the latter part of the third century rather than the early decades of the fourth."

It will be noticed that the above comment contains the words "vocal notes" but how do we know that the signs were for vocal use? It can surely be urged that they are meant to be a guide to the hand of the instrumentalist who may have accompanied the singers, but be it urged and emphasised, not in the modern form and method of accompaniment. I would submit that these signs may well be primitive directives for some instrumentalist, but with such a fragment it is precarious to arrive at any actual decision. However, there is another fragment, even more primitive, mentioned in the Journal of Hellenic Studies (1931, 40V51, p. 100). J. F. Mountford writes in the same journal dealing with this fragment. "We may perhaps have here a famous passage copied out by some Citharode or music student or dilettante for his own purposes; or perhaps this is a draft of some new song in the handwriting of the composer. In any case the fragment was presumably filed among the Zenon Papyri by some mistake; unless, indeed, this piece of music is in some way connected with Heracleotes, the harper, who in two other papyri appeals to Zenon for restitution of his instrument." The conjectural date of this fragment is

B.C. 250—the actual musical signs in question are uncial in character and do not convey a great deal to a musician today, but it is important to note that the editor considers that these uncial signs are connected with the instrumentalist rather than directions in relation to the production of vocal melody. Dr. Wellesz deals very thoroughly with the fragment of the Christian hymn or doxology (p. 125, ff. Hist. Byzantine Music) and although he points out that none of the scholars, who treated the matter of these rhythmical signs at the time of its publication, proceeded to attempt to interpret them, yet Dr. Wellesz certainly offers an interpretation and explanation which is extremely interesting to study but his statement seems more to represent the mind of the present-day composer than the student of musical development in relation to the primitive formulation of a musical technique.

E. A. Wallis Budge points out in "Coptic Biblical Texts (p. xiv) printed for the British Museum, 1912"—"In the Song of Moses (pp. 100ff) there are evidences that an attempt was made to accent parts of the text probably for singing purposes. . . ."

Idelsohn (Jewish Music, p. 27) is more definite. He writes "Music is never written down but transmitted orally. Consequentally 'ear-marks' were developed by which music is recognised. The entire theory of Oriental music is based upon these 'ear-marks', i.e. signs for musical patterns learned by ear." Every word of the foregoing statement is important when considering the process whereby the notation of the 9th century MSS. was compiled. Whether the process was oriental or occidental neither Easterns nor Westerns required to wait upon each other to be taught how to sing. The song of the Folk was universal.

Hence from these "ear-marks" or "accents", perhaps elementary in character in the first instance, greater elaboration would arrive when musical necessity required it. Cantors and precentors in the IXth century may well have been aware of these directive "ear-marks" or even of a much more ancient tradition in relation to instrumental playing. The idea therefore suggested by Dom Sunol, that the IXth Century notation is an elaborated form from a more primitive and perhaps simpler method of notation may be a correct statement.

S. Bede (A.D. 672 or 673-735) mentioning the liturgical missions from Rome which had taken place in Britain, writes— " He received also the aforesaid Abbot John journeying through Britain, since he might teach in his own monastery the year's Cursus for singing as it was rendered at S. Peter's at Rome; and Abbot John did this since he had received the Pontiff's instruction.

hence he taught the cantors of the said Monastery the Order and Rite of singing and reading by word of mouth (Viva Voce Lat :) and those things which the course of the whole year required he also committed to writing." (Plummers Bede Lib : iv. CB. xvi, p. 241).

This passage from Bede is extremely interesting, apparently the instruction in singing and reading was given "Viva Voce" and further reminders were committed to writing, it would be very helpful to know the exact form and appearance of these "reminders". Obviously they dealt with the Text of the Rite but what actual musical signs may have accompanied the said Text it is not possible to decide. There may have been the "ear-marks" already mentioned but the significant words "Viva Voce" suggest a rhythmical rendering free from any limitation imposed by formal notation even of an elementary character.

Before leaving this most fascinating subject it may be well to examine later tendencies and developments in this notational direction. I have already mentioned Dom Sunol (p. 55) who points out how the evolution of the neum continued till the fourteenth century, but Germany continued to use the Chironomic forms. This, of course, would involve a spontaneous flow of vocal melody and with it considerable improvisation. There is clear evidence to show that such practices existed. A scholarly article appeared in the *Musical Quarterly* (January, 1951) by Ernest T. Ferand, where, in a comparatively short article called "Sodaine and Un-expected Music in the Renaissance", the whole question of impro-visation and composition is carefullly investigated. I feel that this matter is not within our terms of reference except to emphasise how free and untrammelled vocal melody continued throughout the ages even within the period of great composers. The written language of music arose as and when artistic necessity required it, but the living melody of the People was always present, not neces-sarily improved when reduced to set forms. In conclusion and in order to illustrate or justify my last sentence I would refer the reader to another article in the *Musical Quarterly* (April, 1949) by Colin McPhee, entitled "The Five-tone Gamelan Music of Bali."

This treatise is invaluable as illustrating the extent of the culture of the Balinese with its foundation on Dance and Song and also the persistence and force of Tradition in National life.

Latin Text, Plummer's Bede, Ch. xvi, p. 241—"Accepit et praefatum Johannem abbatem Brittaniam perducendum; quatenus in monasterio suo cursum canendi annuum sicut ad sanctum

Petrum Romae agebatur edoceret; egitque Abba Johannes, ut canendi ac lengendi Viva Voce praefati monasterii cantores edocendo, et ea, quae totius anni circulus in celebratione dierum festorum poscebat etiam litteris mandando."

CHAPTER V

The Problem of the Romanian Signs

The Problem of the Romanian Signs

WE are now faced with a very interesting problem. When the ninth century MSS were examined at the beginning of the plainsong revival in the latter part of the nineteenth century, certain additional signs or letters appeared in proximity to the chironomic notation and were evidently meant to affect the rendering of the chant : letters like A, L, S, G, apparently denoting an elevation of the voice, others referring to a lowering of pitch, others again relating to rhythm, like C for celeriter, T for ritardando, were all inserted above or near the groups of neum accents. The controversy arising out of the exact interpretation of these signs and of the whole notational grouping became rather acute. There are three schools for interpretation of these signs, known as the Accentualist, the Solesmes, and the Mensuralist schools.* The Accentualists would give equal time value to each syllable of the words and where a melisma occurs the accent then falls on the first note of the neum group. Up to a certain point the Solesmes school would agree but as Gustav Reese points out† "They have discarded the (Accentualist) theory that the verbal accent is the predominating rhythmical element." The late Dom Mocquereau was the leader of the Solesmes school. He not only engaged in exhaustive research but the rendering of the chant under his guidance at Solesmes gave most practical effect to his theories. The beauty of the Solesmes method of chanting is outstanding and can occur anywhere in the world where that system and method are faithfully adhered to when singing the Office. It seems strange if such a result has arisen from a mis-interpretation of history.

---

* Vid.   Gustav Reese: *Music in the Middle Ages*, Dent, U.S.A., and London, Ch. V., p. 140 ff. The whole controversy is very ably and succinctly dealt with by this writer, who seems to favour a Mensuralist solution. The reasons why such an interpretation may be doubtful appear later on in the text of this treatise.

† op. cit.

CHAPTER V

*"The Mensuralists maintain that the Gregorian chant was sung from its beginning up to the twelfth century in measures irregularly grouped, the first note of each measure receiving a stress, and that during this time, therefore, the rhythm of the chant followed the same principles as the rhythm of Eastern music, from which the chant derived." But is not the Mensuralist's theory too largely coloured by the background of present day elaborations of musical technique? Surely there is too much of the "bar line" about it in the modern sense to be a really reliable interpretation of the notation and signs found in the ninth century MSS. It seems difficult in these days for the musician soaked in the great European tradition of music to divest himself of these conditions when trying to interpret remote musical origins. I would challenge the statement I have quoted from Reese's *Music in the Middle Ages* which settles the origin of the chant in the East, I fear the whole burden of this treatise is to confute such a notion. The origin of the chant is to be sought among the singing people of the Catholic Church. The two last words indicate how widespread its nature and character.

*   *   *   *

Looking at the matter from a different angle, what are the rhythmic methods or practices of the folksinger? There is bound to be stress and emphasis in any language when emotion is aroused and this same feeling will express itself in the rhythm of words and melody. Plainsong and folksong are cast in the same modes. But again I must resort to the very obvious remark that the folksinger does not consciously select his mode.† The folksinger today as heretofore makes use of all sorts of colourful emphases, nuances, flowering grace notes. As far back as 1908 Percy Grainger wrote an article in the *Journal of the Folksong Society*§ on collecting folksongs with the phonograph. Studying this article one sees how close the folksinger seems to be to the effects which the early rhythmic sign of the plainchant appears to suggest.

Dealing with the variations, inventiveness and irregularities of the folksinger, Mr. Grainger writes‡: "I find it impossible to render into musical notation anything approaching the full charm of the great or slight rhythmic irregularities ever present in traditional solo singing." Again to show the possible source and reason

---

* op. cit. p. 144.

† Did the Norman Bishops and Abbots instruct their masons to build in the "Norman style" because they came from Normandy?

§ No. 12, Pt. III, Vol. III.

‡ op. cit. p. 152.

for variations in the folksong tradition he continues :* "Frequent uniform repetition of irregularities goes, to my mind, to prove that very many of them are not mere careless or momentary deviations from a normal, regular form, but radical points of enrichment, inventiveness and individualisation evolved in accordance with personal characteristics and hallowed and cemented by consistent usage."

After all the genius of folksong is the full and clear expression of words. The folksinger is absorbed in his story, if it is a ballad, or the emotion called forth by romance or tragedy. We are told all about the incident, clear concise description is given, the melody only adds weight and meaning to the narrative. The chanteyman has to interest his men, in the same way the story and tune have a most definite and important purpose, to make work and therefore life easier and more pleasant. Workers, craftsmen, labourers of every kind have found the very soul of their work in their songs; folksong has called forth some of the highest forms of artistic self-expression. Now if folksong gives such satisfaction to human needs, an outstanding feature which has been known through the ages, it is certainly not unlikely that the charasteristics noticed by musicians of a much later age were observed by those, who in the ninth century were seeking, in a certain sense, to formulate and consolidate the very musical themes, derived from the people, which had definitely found a home within the worship of the Church. It is a case not only of the music but also of all the distinctive methods of rendering it. I would contend that this is what actually happened in the ninth century. Therefore instead of confirming the interpretation of this musical script entirely by appealing to the past, would not present-day folk custom help us better to elucidate what is uncertain and so bridge the gap between the ancient MSS and actual present-day folk practice? While avoiding over-certainty, surely a living contact might thus be made and a lot of trouble and controversy about the significance and interpretation of musical exactitudes be avoided. By way of illustration I must refer again to the letters denoting pause and stress in the the ninth century MSS. The well-known musician Notker interprets the sign G in a most interesting manner, here is the sentence in Latin : "Ut in gutture gradatim garruletur genuine gratulatur."

Now the meaning of this sentence, at first sight, looks rather unintelligible, but I have heard Cecil Sharp say that chanteymen produce a most interesting vocal effect in certain songs, what can only be described as a gurgle in the throat. Can these words of

* op. cit. p. 155.

Notker's be interpreted in the light of this custom? And may not Notker himself be only reproducing a usage of the folksinger as striking to the musician of the ninth century as to the folksong collector of the twentieth? His words might then be translated : "An ascending curve in the form of a gurgle in the throat is genuinely pleasing." Sharp wrote about the folksingers in the Appalachian Mountains : "They have one vocal peculiarity, however, which I have never noticed amongst English folksingers, namely, the habit of dwelling arbitrarily upon certain notes of the melody, generally the weaker accents. This practice, which is almost universal, by disguising the rhythm and breaking up the phrases, produces an effect of improvisation and freedom from rule which is very pleasing." Again I would contend that this occurrence quoted from Sharp's introduction to his *English Folksongs from the Southern Appalachians,* if transferred to the chant, approaches the Solesmes method. Refraining from anything in the nature of certainty, there is surely enough affinity to warrant anyone offering this suggestion. To illustrate my meaning I give the two last phrases of the "Gloria in Excelsis" (in Latin) of the Missa cum Jubilo No. IX of the Vatican Gradual for the Feasts of Our Lady :

I do not attempt to translate the phrase into modern notation although I know crotchets and quavers may seem more intelligible to musicians in these days. It is not fair to the chant to attempt any such proceeding because there is no real identity between the two forms; both have their distinctive spheres, but the rhythm of the chant requires the complete timeless flexibility of the four line stave and the form of the notes as just quoted, what is called the Guidonian notation.

Mr. Gustav Reese quotes three rhythmical interpretations of the Ascensiontide antiphon "Videntibus illis elevatus est", but these three different renderings are given* in modern notation which

---

* *Music in the Middle Ages,* p. 148.

very largely, if not entirely, undermines the whole force of his contention. The words carry their own rhythmical interpretation, the chant accommodating itself to the force and meaning of the words.

The chant, like the folksong, requires the same freedom; I do not wish to suggest that the linguistic methods of the folk are not distinctive, their verbal phrases and vocal effects are for the sake of force and clarity in expression.* Therefore the underlying principle of folksong and plainsong must be identical.

It has been already emphasised that the words of the liturgical text are what really matter. The *Catholic Church* could not do otherwise than turn this ordinary everyday expression of the human soul to higher and extraordinary uses. In the Primitive Ages, any self-conscious mode of expression in the service of the Church would have met with stern condemnation. I must quote a tenth century writer—Hucbold : "Let us abhor every affectation of voice, all ostentation and singularity and whatever calls up the histrionic, nor let us copy those who fling forth the chant too lightly or those who utter the syllables with undue pomposity, let us rather sing every chant with such solemnity yet with such movement, that we sing alway with ease of voice and a full sweet tone."† After all, unselfconscious expression and execution are the base of all true art, it is this characteristic which we most value in folksong and folkdance, its spontaneity appeals, its naturalness is outstanding. These self-same qualities appear in every line of the liturgical text and chant, inspired genius which consecrated to the highest uses what came from the very soul of the people.

---

* Vid. *J. F. S. S.* op. cit. No. 12, Vol. III, p. 167

† From the preface (in English) to the **Vatican Gradual** Edit P.M.M. Soc. 1930, translation by Dom Anselm Hughes.

CHAPTER VI

Variety of Form and Plainsong in the Vernacular

Variety of Form and Plainsong in the Vernacular

So far we have stressed one form of the chant, the Responsorial one, or a group of cantors singing a verse, and the people joining in a refrain, or else responding in the same elaborate fashion, singing the melisma or "in jubilatione". There is another form of the chant where the groups of notes or neums are less ornate, many words of the text being sung to a single note, this is called the Syllabic chant.* After the time of S. Gregory, the chant was shortened, and instead of the primitive method of constant refrain between the verses of the psalms, the psalm would be sung straight through, one side of the choir responding to the other in alternate verses, all joining together at the end in an antiphon which would be appropriate to the occasion or the feast. The music of antiphons, hymns, parts of the Ordinary of the Mass like the Creed, were all syllabic chants. Examples are frequent enough in the Vatican Liber Antiphonarius and the Liber Usualis, English renderings will be found in the English Hymnal. In order to apply in practice what has already been written on rhythmical feeling in the interpretation

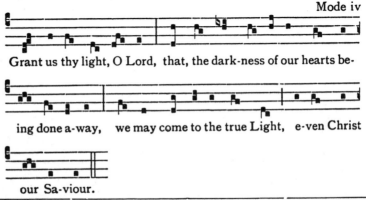

Mode iv

Grant us thy light, O Lord, that, the dark-ness of our hearts be-ing done a-way, we may come to the true Light, e-ven Christ our Sa-viour.

* See note at end of chapter.

of the chant, reference can aptly be made to the English version
of the Sarum Compline by the late Dr. G. H. Palmer. Ant. "Grant
us Thy light, O Lord" :

Examine the whole phrase carefully, notice how sharply the
accented words stand out and how the simple musical phrasing
leads up to a wonderful climax on "Christ", which has only a
single note (punctum) and then a slight curve (torculus) on "our",
making a natural and almost perfect conclusion. This is the case
with all plainsong, where the traditional method has been faithfully followed, down as far as the sixteenth century. Even in the
elaborate chant the same idea is evident, jubilations occur on the
less important words, or, at the end of a word or final syllable,
but here the jubilation is not meant to cover the meaning of the
words, but rather to emphasise that the words called forth the
spirit of joy to such an extent that the feeling could not be expressed
in words, it was more the expression of ecstasy as has been pointed
out in the earlier part of this essay. Is it not this spiritual reality
underlying the unselfconscious expression of all true folksinging
that appealed so strongly to minds like Ambrose or Augustine,
showing the identity, not to say the fusion, of folksong with plainsong?

So far our point of contact is clear, the motive and genius are
the same whatever may be said of the original source of the plainchant. There is one branch of the plainsong, however, which no
less an authority than the late Dr. Wagner maintained, must have
been adopted from folksong and popular melody—the hymn tunes :
"In Syria and Greece hymn music must have approached closely
to the folksong of those countries."* With the other evidence before
us, it would hardly be consistent to think that Syria and Greece
were the only countries where this custom was followed, at all
events the metrical hymns of the fourth and fifth century seem to
have very simple melodies and may well reflect the influence of
another type of folksong.†

By way of illustration, examine the Sarum Compline hymn,
"Cultor Dei memento" :

---

* *Hist. Plainchant,* p, 42, English translation.

† I am indebted to Dom Anselm Hughes for the following note : "The
return of the post-Ambrosians to rhythmic, instead of quantitative,
metre in the hymns of the iambic dimetre points to a return to traditional Italian (as disinct from Graeco-Roman) poetry. All the so-called
classical Latin verse is a Hellenised importation : and if they went back
to pure old Roman method in verse, presumably in music also, I have
held for many years past that, whatever be the origin of the Responsorial
and Psalmodic chants of the Gregorian Cursus, the melodies of the first
cycles of breviary hymns are probably taken over from Italian folksongs."

Mode viij

Servant of God, remember
The hallow'd Font's bedewing;
The Seal of Confirmation,
Thine inner man renewing.

Take heed, when called by slumber,
All chastely thou reclinest,
That with the holy symbol
Thy brow and breast thou signest.

The Cross doth chase all evil
Before it darkness flieth;
That soul abideth steadfast
Which on this Sign relieth.

Far hence! ye wandering phantoms
Of wild unquiet dreaming;
Begone! thou arch-deceiver,
With thine unwearied scheming.

O ever subtil Serpent,
Who toils unnumber'd weavest,
And with thy guileful windings
Our hearts of peace bereavest,

Avaunt! for Christ is with us,
Yea, Christ is here, then vanish!
This Sign—full well thou knowst it—
Can all thy legions banish.

What though the weary body
Awhile its rest be taking,
The soul shall, e'en in slumber,
To thoughts of Christ be waking.

Laud to the Sire Eternal,
To Christ, true King of Heaven,
And Paraclete most holy,
Be now and ever given.*

There are many wonderful hymn melodies, but none can
surely surpass this melody for beauty of tone, ease of flexion and
a straightforward simplicity which give meaning and value to every

* Latin version: p. 68.

line of the text. It may seem a bold statement, but I would venture
to state that Dr. Palmers translation appears to improve the
original and therefore enhance the phraseology of both words and
music.* Nobody can surely say, after hearing this hymn sung, that
plainsong was only meant to be sung in Latin—one might as well
assert that folksong is only suited for one language or dialect.
Perhaps this last statement contains something in the nature of a
challenge which therefore requires further justification. The writer
of this treatise has found the opinion continually repeated that
the plainchant is only rhythmically and verbally suited for a
Latin liturgy. Even when it is pointed out that folksongs are found
in practically every country sung in exactly the same musical
theme as the Gregorian modes, none the less the contrary view
seems to be persistently held.† It is therefore interesting to study
Dom Gregory Murray's article in some detail as an illustration of
that persistence already referred to in the previous sentence.

I sincerely hope I am not misunderstanding Dom Gregory's
standpoint; his contention seems to centre round the difference
between English and Latin verbal accent. Hence he contends that
the melodic accent of the chant cannot be fitted into an English
verbal phrase. For instance, the final sentence of the Nicene Creed
where, in Latin, the verbal accent is, as it were, retarded : "Et
vítam ventúri saéculi.", and in English where the accent is thrown
forward : "And the lífe of the wórld to cóme"—but surely, the
whole flexibility of the chant, like the modal folksong, lends itself
to this change of language? Here is the musical phrase with both
the Latin and English words, and where is the essential difference?

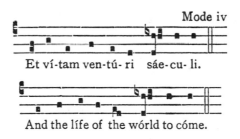

Mode iv

Et ví-tam ven-tú- ri sáe-cu- li.

And the lífe of the wórld to cóme.

Again, Dom Gregory quotes the English version of the Rorate
Caeli in the English Hymnal (735) to establish his contention by
a further example of false accentuation. In the first place, I cannot agree that this particular melody represents a good example

* See Latin version at end of chapter.
† Vid. *Downside Review*, April, 1947. Article by Dom Gregory Murray,
"Plainsong and a Vernacular Liturgy."

of the chant or that it is really fair to give the melody in modern notation as it appears in the *Downside Review*. Here is the music and words given in the English Hymnal:

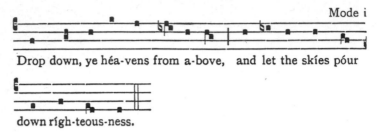

Mode i

Drop down, ye héa-vens from a-bove, and let the skíes póur

down rígh-teous-ness.

Dom Gregory comments: "Could anything be more unnatural than the setting of the accented "skies" to a single note, followed by two notes on the weak "pour", and similarly of the first two syllables of "righteousness"? In each case the verbal accent has a single note on the up-beat and is immediately followed by a weak syllable coinciding with the musical ictus and adorned with a group of notes—a procedure which English will not bear." It is difficult to understand what this statement really means because the words of significance and therefore the emphasis are on "heavens" and "pour", the music naturally adapts itself to this situation.* It is more difficult still to follow Dom Gregory's explanation of the spondaic and dactylic "pattern" in accentuation. In ecclesiastical Latin, rhythmic prose or verse does not consider quantitative measure as represented by the dactyl and the spondee, quantity has given place to accent, any contention arising from this particular standpoint of the unsuitability of English plainsong could not be sustained. Again, I join issue with Dom Gregory, rather more decidedly this time, when he writes: "There is an important difference between the general structure of English and of Latin and the plainsong technique is directly derived from the Latin, whose natural music it is."

What are the grounds for this statement? In the first instance, I very much question its validity. Greek must be considered as well as Latin; Syriac, too, with Hebrew may have played their part, not to mention other forms of folk dialect and therefore

---

* I must refer here to what A. Robertson has written in *The Interpretation of Plainchant*, Oxford Univ. Press, p. 17: " I have spoken so far of musical accent, but we need not assume warfare between this and the verbal accent of the text to which the music is allied. In syllabic chant (one syllable=one note) all agree that the music receives its rhythm from the words so that if the text is binary or ternary or if it be mixed, the music will follow suit. The note lengths are indeterminate in that they vary according to the time required to enunciate the syllables."

universal folksong.* Surely the whole matter, under immediate discussion, revolves round a question of taste and bias. An idea takes root and becomes deeply embedded and hereafter reasons are sought to establish a position, which more mature study and experience might show to be untenable. I feel this is the case with English plainsong; when dealing with the Modal System, the safest method of study and criticism is from the angle of the music of the people, the folksong.

I am quite ready to grant to Dom Gregory a personal preference for Latin plainchant. Latin contains more perfect and evenly-spaced vowel sounds which lend themselves to the singing voice and also the articulation of the consonants. Using the chant in Latin, you certainly avoid the English "th", "st" and final "g", which may serve to weaken clear enunciation and smooth diction. But long experience has taught me that plainsong avoids rather than accentuates these linguistic difficulties.

The intense rhythmic beauty underlying such a work as the late Dr. Palmer's Psalter has only to be studied and heard to be appreciated, and after all, the spiritual life of many Anglican Religious centres round the Office Books, in English, which Dr. Palmer edited. The English words are the vehicle for the soul's expression and where language means so much, the chant in English does not fail to be the medium for supplying a heartfelt spiritual need.†

A final word about the flexibility of the chant. Dr. Palmer adhered to what is known as the "abrupt mediation" when rendering certain tones.§ That is, where certain notes of the music would be redundant owing to the shortness of the verbal phrase the full mediation is omitted.

Mode viij

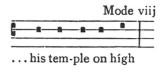

. . . his tem-ple on high

---

* Vid. *Incident in the life of S. Aldhelm*, p. 84.

† If I may write without presumption, perhaps Dom Gregory might reconsider what he has written if he heard, as I do, Sunday by Sunday Norfolk country children sing with Norfolk intonation the Kyrie, Sanctus and Agnus in English plainchant. Or again, as I heard quite recently, French children at the Parish Church at Garches, near Paris, led by the Curé, engage in a dialogue Mass and sing in "French Plainchant" the Agnus Dei. Does this latter effort represent the New Liturgical Movement?

§ Vid. *Plainsong Psalter*, p. xi.

This practice has been abandoned in the Latin psalter, hence you find at times rather strained renderings such as in the "De profundis" (Psalm 129):

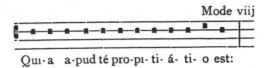

Mode viij

Qui- a a-pud té pro-pi- ti- á- ti- o est:

Dr. Palmer considered this method not to be truly euphonic and did not agree with the abandonment of the "mediatio correpta" which helped to smooth still further any possible conflict between words and music. Perhaps the English rendering here would have a certain verbal and melodic advantage.

NOTE I

I HAVE been rather disturbed by certain statements about the chant made by Dom Gregory Dix in his otherwise profound study of the *Shape of the Liturgy*. On p. 141 in a footnote he writes that the ferial tone for the preface in the missal represents the primitive form of the chant, the implication being that the syllabic form of the chant is more primitive than the melismatic. It has been fairly fully pointed out in this essay that the evidence does not support this view. The responsorial chant and the Alleluia were as familiar to the people as the syllabic chant. All the congregation in turn took their part in the liturgy. Vide Tertullian (Lib: II, Ad Uxorem, Ch. IX, Patr: Vol. 1, p. 1302) who certainly seems to support this statement. His words addressed to a husband are "Sonant inter duos psalmi et hymni et mutuo provocant quis melius deo suo canet." Translation: "Psalms and hymns flow forth between them mutually encouraging one another, who will sing a better theme to God." Also see Gerbert "De Cantu et Musica Sacra", Vol. I, p. 61, who discusses the question of primitive congregational worship with patristic references. It is therefore more surprising to read (p. 442): "At the pre-Nicene synaxis a passive part was all that was possible for the congregation. . . ." Does Dom Gregory really think that the faithful did not join in the psalmody because they were unable to sing the jubilations of the chant? I feel inclined to refer Dom Gregory to p. 198 (op. cit.) where he warns us against "modern presuppositions". Again his criticism (p. 366) of the method of selection in past ages in regard to the Propers seems equally open to criticism and also the rather severe strictures he makes on account of the "musical obsessions and liturgical tiresomeness of some choirmen throughout all ages." It is also difficult to see why the Offertory for the 21st Sunday after Pentecost should be considered inappropriate, it is after all a brief summary of what is read at Matins on the first two Sundays in September according to the Monastic Rite and may well reflect remote liturgical practice in reference to the use of the book of Job.

Again on p. 365 Dom Gregory refers to the "difficult neumatic notation of the day." If he means the chironomic notation of a MS like the S. Gall codex, it is doubtful if this musical text was ever difficult to follow since it was obviously compiled to help the singers. In all these matters to which I have made reference, there is an uncomfortable feeling that a modern mentality is thrusting an equally modern interpretation on ancient Catholic schemes of worship where the motives underlying past actions are quite outside the range of our present-day thinking.

I must carry this notion a little further when considering what Dom Gregory says (p. 618) about the cultural level of the mediaeval people. I do not think Dom Gregory means to disparage the civilisation of the Middle Ages, but to talk about the "dialectical differences and linguistic poverty of the great mass of the people in each country were still much too great for national vernacular liturgies to have been a practicable proposition," to say the least is unfortunate because it is an inaccurate statement. Furthermore an even more questionable suggestion is offered (p. 619) where "the great half-submerged mass of the population was just beginning to be articulate." Does this mean that the folk in any age or in any country were ever inarticulate? The real traditions of a people are found in the minds and memories of the unlettered folk whose power to remember and hand on to succeeding generations is unrivalled. The very fact that the folk can neither read nor write means that their memories are enhanced to a degree far exceeding our educated faculties. So caution is necessary before statements are made about the dialectal or linguistic incapacity of people who may be unlettered, but still through song and dance and their resulting colourful movements, show a far greater power of natural self-expression than the self-consciously educated in any age.

I feel it has been really necessary to draw attention, with all due emphasis, to these matters, but none the less I look on Dom Gregory's work as a study of first-rate importance and wish to hear record with gratitude to the scholarly research and trouble which his book, the *Shape of the Liturgy,* must have entailed

* * * *

NOTE II (see p. 62).

Latin version

Cultor Dei memento
Te fontis et lavacri
Rorem subiisse sanctum
Te Chrismate innovatum.

Fac, cum vocante somno
Castum petis cubile
Frontem locumque cordis
Crucis figura signet.

Crux pellit omne crimen
Fugiunt crucem tenebrae
Tali dicata signo
Mens fluctuare nescit.

Procul O Procul vagantum
Portenta somniorum
Procul esto pervicaci
Praestigiator astu.

O tortuose Serpens
Qui mille per maeandros
Fraudesque flexuosas
Agitas quieta corda.

Discede Christus hic est,
Christus hic est, liquesce,
Signum quod ipse nosti
Damnat tuam catervam.

Corpus licet fatiscens
Taceat reclive paululum
Christum tamen sub ipso
Meditabitur sopore.

Gloria aeterno Patri
Et Christo vero regi
Paraclitoque sancto
Et nunc et in perpetuum.   Amen

CHAPTER VII

The Jewish Musical Tradition

CHAPTER   VII

The Jewish Musical Tradition

MENTION has been made in the previous chapter concerning the reiteration of opinions about the source and use of the chant for rather inadequate reasons. This criticism applies to the subject matter of the present chapter—the Jewish musical tradition. Dr. Egon Wellesz states in the *American Musical Quarterly* (July, 1947): "The kernel of the melodies of both the Eastern and Western Churches derived from the melodies of the Jewish Synagogue." Now it requires a certain boldness, if not temerity, to question Wellesz's opinion on such a matter, but it is surely allowable to consult definite Jewish authority before coming to any final conclusion. The Rev. Paul Levertoff* states that "there is no mention of singing at the synagogue", adding, however, the probability that parts of the liturgy connected with the Temple worship would be sung. This view by a former Jewish authority hardly coincides with anything in the nature of a settled tradition of chanting in the Synagogue, or any method of singing psalms, lessons or benedictions which could have been borrowed or handed over to the Christian Synagogue or congregation in the first or second century. I applied to the above writer for further confirmation and he kindly wrote: "I can only confirm the fact that in Rabbinic literature there is no mention of singing in the early synagogue. One must, however, take into consideration the fact that the reading of the Law and the Prophets in the Synagogue, not to speak of the accompanying benedictions, were spoken rhythmically." This last word rhythmically is precisely the crux of the whole question, the reader spontaneously broke into natural melody, and this clearly follows out later synagogic practice which seems to have followed no definite or technical system of chanting. One has in mind at this juncture purely original sources in the first four Christian centuries. When contact is made with later

* *Liturgy and Worship*, S.P.C.K., p. 66.

70

ages the questions relative to the origin of the melodies sung in Jewish Synagogues seems to be beyond doubt. The whole matter is treated learnedly in two articles in the *Jewish Encyclopaedia*, the first deals with cantillation, the Jewish counterpart of our central theme the jubilation. The writer of the article says : "The cantillation adheres only to modes similar to those of the Byzantine and Armenian traditions, of the folksong of Eastern Europe and of Perso-Arab melody. This modal feeling of Jewish worship music is still reminiscent of the musical theory and practice of Eastern Asia which radiated from Babylon to the Mediterranean and to the Indian Ocean."

The same writer* has an even more illuminating article on Music in relation to Synagogue Worship, tracing various phases through which the tradition has passed, showing its modal significance and its indebtedness to the singing customs of the people, gentile as well as Jew, in the particular locality where they were situated. In fact, where traditional methods were more definitely standardized, the said methods were the outcome of conscious and unconscious borrowing from the same original source. "Besides the traditional material of such actual Jewish origin and development, there has been preserved in the music of the synagogue a considerable mass of melody directly adapted from the folksong of gentile neighbours or constructed on the general lines of musical development in the outer world." †

The same writer again in a further essay,§ shows how the Synagogue worship came under the influence of the metrical hymn which has happened since the eighth century. The melodies adopted were folksong in origin. Mr. Cohen writes in the same essay in relation to the musical methods employed "in order to make it certain what tune was to be used, the adaptor often would commence his new hymn with Hebrew words, either signifying the same as those of the folksong for the tune of which he was writing, or even actually reproducing in sound the original secular text, of course with a great difference in the meaning." ‡

---

* F. L. Cohen : Jewish Encyclopaedia : Arts : "Cantillation" and "Music". Mention of the Indian Ocean makes me refer to very interesting articles by Arthur Hutchings in *Music and Letters*, *Music in Bengal*, January, 1946, and *Indian Traditions, Classical and Popular*, April, 1946, 2 vols.

† F. L. Cohen, ibid.

§ *Folksong Survivals in Jewish Worship-Music*. paper read to the English Folksong Society, November 23rd, 1899, by the Rev. F. L. Cohen.

‡ Vid. the musical illustrations given on pp. 52-59 of the same Journal, Vol. I, No. 2, 1900.

My plea is, arising from the foregoing Jewish quotations, that although Christian worship originally centred round the Law, the Prophets and the Psalms besides the Gospels, Epistles and other New Testament writings, yet we cannot urge that there was any "fixed" system or standard which the Synagogue "handed" on to the Church. Such an idea seems entirely alien to both Jewish and Christian method. When the Christian Communities separated and diverged from Jewish influence, Primitive Catholicism became sharply antagonistic to Judaism,* and the Christian appeal found response not among Jews, but among the unlettered folk, slaves, freedmen and labourers throughout the Roman Empire, it would be in these sections of society where we should look for a musical tradition. Surely we are led to exactly the same conclusion in relation to this Jewish musical tradition as we are to the plain-song of the Church.

Whether this music reflects the influence of the Temple or the local Synagogue, it is indigenous and has been borrowed from the people of the place where the Jewish community is settled and exhibits the characteristics of their environment. Following the course of the development of the music in Synagogue worship, it seems to be nothing more than the evolution of the folksong. As we find a distinctive character in the Roman, Ambrosian, Gallican or Mozarabic tradition of the plainchant, so with the Synagogue we find Ashkenazic, a Northern and Eastern European form, Sephardic (Spanish) or Southern form.

If there appears outstanding activity in the Christian Church (viz. in the ninth century), similar influences appear in the Synagogue because both institutions were receiving inspiration, or motif, from the same source—the folksinger.

I hope sufficient evidence has been forthcoming to show that the music-worship of the Jewish Synagogue was too indefinite to have had anything in the nature of systematic influence on plain-chant of the Catholic Church.†

---

* Vid. Ep: Hebr. 13, vers. 10 Mgr. Knox's trans.. "We have an altar of our own, and it is not those who carry out the worship of the tabernacle that are qualified to eat its sacrifices."

† The two articles mentioned, *Cantillation* and *Music* in the *Jewish Encyclopaedia*, by the Rev. F. L. Cohen, are well worth careful study, both for their content and the musical illustrations the author gives, but he is surely in error on p. 121 of his article on music when he states: "The Church plainsong never developed the rapid and florid ornamentation of the synagogue hazzanut (i.e., the art of the hazzan or cantor) because of the early development of choral participation in the church service." As we have seen in the quotation from Cassiodorus (q.v.) extremely florid methods of responsorial singing were employed by the laity which was the universal Christian practice.

NOTES

Jubilatio and ἀλαλαγμός
(Brown, Driver and Briggs, *Hebrew Lexicon,* Oxford Univ. Press, pg. 929). Equivalents of two Hebrew nouns:

יְלָלָה,   +   תְּרוּעָה
yelalah   +   teru'ah
(1)   (2)

from two verbs: לל, יָלַל   +   רוּע

יָלַל   (onomatopoeic):   to howl, to make a howling noise
(1) of distress. Hosea 7. *14*.
(2) of exultation. Isaiah 52. *5*.

ἀλαλαγμός   only used once for the word Jeremiah 32. *26* (LXX)
רוּע   (1) to raise a shout.
(2) to give a blast on a clarion or horn.
Hosea 5. *8*.
(3) to shout in triumph over enemies.
Jer. 50. *15*.
Psalm 41. *12*.
(4) to shout in applause. Zach. 9. *9*.
(5) to shout with religious impulse.
1 Sam. 4. *5*. (When ark was brought into camp of Israelites).
LXX   ἀλαλαγμός.
(6) shout for joy in harvest.
The valleys and meadows in Psalm 65. *14*. "laugh and sing".
κεκράζονται και ὑμνήσουσιν.
Latin="clamabunt etenim hymnum dicent."

תְּרוּעָה   (a) used too of shout of joy in public worship.
"He shall pray unto God and shall see His face with joy." Job 33. *36*.
Vulgate: et videbit faciem eius in jubilo.
LXX: εἰσελευσεται προσωπωπω ἱλαρῳ συν ἐζηγοριᾳ.

also: Psalm 33. *3*. "Sing praises unto him lustily with a good courage."
Vulgate: bene psallite ei in vociferatione.
LXX: καλῶς ψάλατε (αὐτω) ἐν ἀλαλαγμῳ.
Psalm 47: sing praises and sing praises. . .
Vulgate: psallite.
LXX: ψαλατε.

also :   (b) of joyful singing in general.
Job. 8. *21.* "Till he fill thy lips with
rejoicing."
Vulgate : ". . . et labia tua jubilo."
LXX : τα κειλη αυτων εζομολογήσεως.

Further note illustrative of A. Z. Idelsohn's book " Jewish
Music in its Historical Development" (Tudor Publishing Co., New
York) : this book requires a separate note since it is a work of
outstanding importance.

After a careful study of its contents I feel I have little to add
to the main theme of this Chapter or to my contention as to the
source of the Ecclesiastical Chant in relation to the Music worship
of the Synagogue. Idelsohn is in no possible doubt about the
original source both of the Music and song of the Temple and
the Synagogue. "The vocal song of the Temple, like all religious
song among the ancient and primitive nations, drew its sap from
folksong." (op. cit. p. 20). Again (p. 27), "Oriental music has
retained the folk-character." "Music is never written down but
transmitted orally."

Writing of the "Biblical Modes", he says, "They are of an
ancient age, probably preceding the expulsion of the Jewish people
from Palestine, and older than the Christian Church. They are
the remainder of the Jewish Palestinian folk tunes, representing
the Jewish branch of the Semitic-Oriental song" (p. 71). And of
the source and origin he writes : ". . . the originality of a national
music is not dependant upon an original scale, but upon original
motives and melodic curves which above all express the characteristics of a nation, a group, or a people." (p. 87).

The whole of Idelsohn's work is a mine of information both
as a general survey of the subject and as the most careful and
critical treatment of the matter in detail. He makes some slight
inaccuracies when dealing with the Ecclesiastical Chant since he
relies on the rather uncritical judgment of certain writers. For
instance, he refers to the later Dr. Wagner's opinion that the
source of the Chant came from the Synagogue rather than the
people. An idea which runs counter to everything he states about
the source of the music worship of the Synagogue. The conclusion
is, of course, obvious, if the source from which Synagogue music
arises is from the Folk, and the Catholic Church adopted this
method, then both systems must have had the same common origin.
But it seems difficult to believe that the first non-Jewish Christians
were "tone-deaf" or "tongue-tied" in the matter of vocal expres-

sion or had to wait for a "Jewish song sheet"(!) before they could create and carry forward a musical tradition.

I have made reference to primitive origins. As the ages advance there is no question that the music of the Synagogue turned again and again to the Folksong for immediate use with or without adaptation. Even as late as the eighteenth and nineteenth centuries the custom arose among Christian as well as Jewish congregations of rescuing and sublimating folk melodies from the power of the "Devil" and using them for religious and spiritual purposes. A casual glance at Idelsohn's invaluable history will certainly confirm this statement. (Vide: Idelsohn Hist: J. M. Pt. II, p. 357 ff).

CHAPTER VIII

The Ninth Century
The Tropes

The Ninth Century
The Tropes *

THE introduction of the tropes in the ninth and tenth centuries
had lasting influence on the whole evolution of European musical
and dramatic art. It is uncertain what the word actually means,
but we have already seen it used as a musical term applied to
singing on vowel sounds or "in jubilatione" in the sixth century.
A trope is actually setting words to these notes of the jubilation,
a trope is a verbal and musical interpolation in the actual text
of the liturgy lengthening out the words of the text considerably.

Notker,† who has already been mentioned, has been wrongly
credited with being the author of this treatment of the Alleluia
sung between the Epistle and the Gospel, but the same method
was applied to other parts of the Liturgy where elaborate groups
of neums existed. Dealing with the sequence or prose form,
Clemens Blume, S. J. points out§ that although the Alleluia jubilus
is supposed to form the basis of the melody, yet in reality it differs
from this jubilus both in length and kind. He writes: "The introduction, it is true, follows the melody of its Alleluia; a few words
that follow are frequently adapted to the first notes of the melisma
to the Gregorian Alleluia, but the melody of the sequence then
entirely deserts the melisma of the Alleluia and never returns to it."

---

* See Introduction to the Winchester Troper (H.B. Society), edit. W. H.
Frere. Discussing the influence of the people's music on this new development of the Church's chant, Dr. Frere defines folksong as "the
spontaneous outflow of the untutored soul of the people."

† I have again to thank Dom Anselm for the following note: "Notker is
not the originator of the trope and sequence (in its historical and literary
sense) cf. Clark: *The Monastery of S. Gall,* or Bannister, Intro. to Vol.
LIII *Analecta Hymnica,* Dreves and Blume. The origin is Norman
French and the Jumièges legend is coming to be substantiated by the
gradual appearance of evidence." Vide Intro, to Winchester Troper ut
supra.

§ *Catholic Encyclopaedia,* Art. "Prose."

It must, too, be remembered, that vocal music at this time was a very living thing, therefore the exact nature of this situation can hardly be over emphasised when compared with the position today. It seems merely pedantic to refer to this situation again, but none the less, we have to divert our minds entirely from the consequences of printing, radio, the multiplicity of pianos and all the mechanical contrivances that pass for music in this century. Music, at the time we are dealing with, was very largely vocal, as Dr. Frere has said : "It was the spontaneous outflow of the unlettered folk." Hence these proses and sequences are something like what Dr. Wagner described : "A sort of reaction of folksong against the sublime art of the Church." It is difficult to say why he used the word against, when the position seems more like the main stream of a river picking up a very helpful tributary. There is no formal artistic need or obligation for the Alleluia Jubilus to correspond to the text of the sequence, we may be quite sure the peasants in the ninth century were still singing in the manner described by S. Augustine in the fourth century.

The late Dr. Eileen Power tells a very interesting story about the ninth century when the knowledge of the chant is considered to be at the height of its reputation for beauty of tone and execution.* "Once when a clerk was singing the Alleluia in the Emperor Charlemagne's presence, Charles turned to one of the bishops : "My clerk is singing very well," whereat the rude bishop replied : "Any clown in our countryside drones as well as that to his oxen at their ploughing." It might be rightly urged that this bishop was not only a keen critic but possessed very considerable musical insight.†

Again there is a fascinating story from the life of S. Aldhelm in the seventh century which comes through King Alfred in the ninth century down to William of Malmesbury in the twelfth century, who describes the incidents, giving King Alfred as his authority.§

"Therefore being well learned, he‡ did not neglect the songs of his native tongue, so that, as Alfred bears witness, of whom I

---

* Eileen Power : *Mediaeval People*, p. 11.
† Vid. append. p. 117 for an account of the whole story and for a reconsideration of Dr. Power's rendering of the original text.
§ I am indebted to Dr. John Powell's preface to Dr. Pullen Jackson's *Spiritual Folksongs of Early America* for this reference but I traced out the entire quotation in the Rolls series which is so important for the matter in hand that I have made a full translation. Vide William of Malmesbury : *Gesta Pontificum*, Rolls Series, 1870, edit. N.E.S.A., Hamilton, pp. 336, 190, Lib. V.
‡ S. Aldhelm.

have spoken above, no one of his own age was ever equal to him. He made English poetry and collected songs, he was equally apt in singing and speaking. Finally Alfred calls to mind a rude song, which is still commonly sung that Aldhelm made, showing the reason why he clearly proves that he only saw in those things which may seem to be frivolous are really the reverse (institisse). The semi-barbarous people at that time by no means intent on the word of God were wont when Mass was sung to run off home.* Therefore the holy man stood on a bridge which connected the country and the town, as people were going out he placed himself as a barrier like a professional gleeman. More than once he attracted the special favour and attention of the crowd. By this device he gradually inserted the words of the Scriptures into the frivolous songs, thereby bringing back the citizens to a healthy state of mind : whom, if he had thought to deal with them severely and with excommunication he would assuredly have done nothing."

Coupled with other evidence, this story may certainly be genuine if only through the impression which the personality of Aldhelm seems to have made on the minds of his fellow countrymen. However, we will move on to a later period and tell another story, this time from the thirteenth century. The late Dr. G. G. Coulton, in his book *From S. Francis to Dante* (Ch. IX) quoting Salimbene's Chronicle, writes of one Bro. Henry of Pisa, a learned man and a marvellous singer. "Having heard a certain maid servant tripping through the Cathedral of Pisa singing in the vulgar tongue :

"If thou carest not for me
I will care no more for thee.'

He made then after the pattern of that, words and music of this hymn following :

"Christ divine, Christ of mine,
Christ the King and Lord of all."

What was taking place in one country, as far as worship was concerned, might well react in other directions; vocal and singing customs in relation to the Divine Office might differ in ceremonial details but fundamentally they are similar. Again the instance of the Rota—Sumer is icumen in—is a clear case in point and emphasises Salimbene's story of Bro. Henry of Pisa. The Rota, if not a folksong, has the theme and characteristics of a folksong. The original MS contains interpolated ecclesiastical words in Latin evidently showing that the scribe was determined to see that the

---

* Lat. "Domos cursitare." We find this particular Anglo-Saxon tradition still persisting in spite of S. Aldhelm !

"Opus Dei" must share in such attractive harmony, thereby anti-cipating the practices both Christian and Jewish, of much later ages.

But the Rota is not a unique occurrence; through interest and patient research further instances are coming to light. In the *Times* issue of 10th February 1955 the Athens correspondent reported:—

"The musical symbols on a set of thirteen Greek folk songs dating from the fifteenth or early sixteenth century have now been deciphered and provide, according to some authorities here, the missing link between the Greek folksong and the Byzantine liturgical chant, the musical connection of which with the Greek hymns of classical times has, apparently, been established. This would prove that there has been an unbroken line in the musical history of Greece from ancient times to the present day".

The codex in question is in the library at Mount Athos. As far as I know there was no further public notice of this important discovery till 19th November 1959 when articles appeared in the *Listener* by John Leatham and Professor Wellesz. Mr. Leatham describes the history of the discovery in some detail and Professor Wellesz has to acknowledge the "closeness" of Byzantine sacred and secular music, "just as some Western troubadour songs are closely related to plainchant melodies". But this relationship is not only found amongst the troubadours; the Folksong, one might claim, the "cry" of the unlettered folk the world over was surely the right basis for the "worship" foundation of the Christian Assembly and ultimately the source which inspired the later great musicians. Christian people did not wait to be instructed by the Synagogue or any other extraneous organisation—may we not record again that they sang because singing was their chief means of spiritual self-expression.

The development of the plainchant and the introduction of the tropes in the ninth century represent a distinct musical and rhythmical process which arose out of the position of the Catholic Church in world affairs, and the peculiar circumstances of the evolution of these events.

Europe by the ninth century was beginning to feel the effects of the new Catholic culture founded largely on monastic ideals. Fundamental human urges were seeking self-expression through new channels, the form must be the worship of the Church, but the medium was an entirely original sense of music and drama. It was this "trope singing", the desire for more extensive verbal utterance, the introduction of dialogue and the popular and colloquial character of these tropes which not only gained appreciation but resulted in wide and varied dramatic treatment. It is not necessary to deal with this side of the question because it has already been dealt with very extensively,* but it must be remembered that the movement arose entirely on a musical basis. A foundation which had its inspiration in folksong as much in the ninth century as in the fourth. Two branches of musical art make their appearance, musical harmony and liturgical drama. Looking over the pages of one of the ancient tropers, it is fascinating to think of the extent of the cultural influence which resulted from this ninth century development, precentors required greater exactitude, they were no longer patient with doubtfulness of pitch. Cottonius (*circa* 1050), is reported to have said : "The same marks which Master Trudo sang as thirds, were sung as fourths by Master Albinus, while Master Salamo asserts that fifths were intended." These remarks throw light on the presence of the "organa" in the Winchester Troper. The organa is the beginning of harmony or more strictly, diaphony, that is, early part music. what at a later period would be known as descant. The early attempts may have been straightforward enough. The late Dr. Frere points out† :

"To sing at the interval of an octave needs no science at all, and so long as the musician kept himself to the tetrachord system there was no difficulty as to diaphony at the fifth above or below, for the melody took exactly the same form only in another tetrachord; but at any other interval the melody was liable to be transformed through being transferred to a different collocation of tones and semi-tones. The above-mentioned treatises (*Musica Enchiriadis* and *Scholiae Enchiriadis*) pointed this out and then went on to give rules for the combining of two organa for the one principalis and for modifying the symphonia diatesseron, or diaphony at the fourth, so as to avoid harshness. This modification is the first step towards real harmony as opposed to a mere reproduction of the same melody at another pitch; and as soon as it appeared the organum became, not a mere mechanical repetition of the principalis, but another part more or less independent of it in as much as, though following its progressions slavishly in the main, it diverged at times to avoid an ugly chord. Another form of modification also had to be made owing to the limitation of the downward range of the "vox organalis" and this by develop-

---

* Vid.. E. K. Chambers: *The Mediaeval Stage.*
† Introduction to the Winchester Troper (H.B.S.) p. xxxviii.

ing the principle of a pedal—also led in the same direction towards real and free harmony, one part standing still while the other moved. Here we have practically the principles of similar and oblique motion in germ."

It is well to quote this passage at length because it explains succinctly the effect of the organa on the future development of harmony. It was almost inevitable that the unrestricted freedom of the chant with its handmaid folksong would have to submit to the creative ability of the skilled musician with his enhanced sense of tone. Study and arrangement, method and organisation, were the obvious necessities, hence arose what has already been stated, the interpretation of popular song in the terms of art formulae. But whatever form the process took, perhaps not always wise in expression, none the less for very many centuries there was still the original source from which to draw.

The art musician in the ninth, thirteenth or sixteenth centuries knew where to look for inspiration.

It has been suggested that the Church adopted organum from folk-polyphony* and if polyphony why not unisonal singing as well? Our own country dancers know too that John Playford could not have produced a "Dancing Master" of permanent value without the agelong experience of the song and dance of the common folk.

I have already mentioned the need of greater collaboration between the lovers of folk music and those to whom plainsong is still a living spiritual experience. In the ninth century MSS we have enshrined, not only a liturgical chant, but a vital folk tradition and method of singing which has actually survived to the present day. By treating both traditions as a parallel study, it is possible to discover a sound basis for their mutual interpretation.

---

* Gustav Reese: *Music in the Middle Ages,* p. 294.

CHAPTER IX

The Immediate Relationship Between Folksong and Plainsong

The Question of Tonality

CHAPTER IX

The Immediate Relationship Between
Folksong and Plainsong

The Question of Tonality

IN 1938 Dr. Herman Reichenbach wrote an article in *Music and Letters* on the tonality of English and Gaelic folksong. This statement is most valuable because it is a practical endorsement of the main contention of this treatise. Dr. Reichenbach has made, within the compass of a magazine article, a very exact analysis of the whole modal system underlying the musical technique of the chant. Furthermore he draws into his method of comparison a number of our best-known English modal folksongs. His knowledge is exact and his criticism precise, so it is difficult to attempt to summarise his conclusions, but there is no question, if the above writer is correct in his statement, that the plainsong of the Church is the folksong of the people.

Dr. Reichenbach gives very useful musical comparisons but with all respect to his wide musical knowledge I feel that to illustrate the modal tonality of a folksong with reference only to a psalm tone is not quite sufficient. I therefore give a Dorian song, "I'm seventeen come Sunday", and follow it first with an antiphon in the first mode, and then the first tone for the psalm in full with the fifth ending. Similarly I have treated the "White Pater Noster" in the Phrygian or third mode, and "William Taylor" in the Mixolydian or seventh mode.

Finally with definite presumption I give a "new" scheme for a Kyrie. I do so with the thought in my mind of the origin of the chant for the Kyrie of the "Missa Rex Splendens" (Sarum and Vatican Gradual) which legend claims S. Dunstan heard the angels sing; the authenticity of this story I am not here to examine or dispute, but I submit that Charlemagne's bishop already quoted might have given, if consulted, a slightly different explanation.

In my examples and illustrations I have adopted an unusual course. The melodies are written on a stave of four lines and in twelfth or thirteenth century notation. This apparent anomaly is not an antiquarian conceit because I feel unaccompanied singing, like folksong and plainsong, requires complete and entire freedom and flexibility. Only the plainchant notation can make this feature secure. Furthermore an old monastic friend and cantor once told me he found the chironomic notation of S. Gall more helpful, when singing, than the later Guidonian notation.

I do not mean music should stop dead at the twelfth century, yet one wonders if the introduction of the bar line has really helped polyphony, and if we are interpreting the ancient composers correctly by inserting the rhythmic exactitudes of our modern musical technique. I only offer these suggestions with extreme caution, knowing well what a rock of offence I may be setting up on which the unwary may well be rent asunder.

Although the following matter is really outside my sphere of interest, yet I must refer to one of Eric Blom's articles in the *Observer* on February 21st, 1954, the title is :— Musical Techniques. Mr. Blom is commenting on a lecture given by Alan Bush to the Composers' Concourse, which dealt with "present-day problems of musical theory". I think this lecture and the criticism which it called forth helps to justify the suggestion I have made in the text about this uncertainty of interpretation.

Dorian

As I walked out one May morn-ing, One May morn-ing so ear-ly, I ov-er-took a hand-some maid, Just as the sun was ris-ing, With my rue dum day, Fol the did-dle dol, Fol the dol the did-dle dum the day.

Mode i. 5

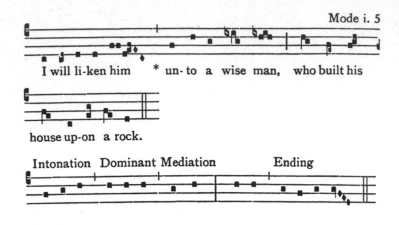

I will li-ken him   * un- to a wise man,   who built his

house up-on a rock.

Intonation Dominant Mediation   Ending

Mode i

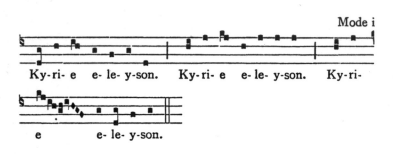

Ky-ri- e   e- le- y-son.   Ky-ri- e   e- le- y-son.   Ky-ri-

e   e- le- y-son.

Phrygian

Mat-thew, Mark and Luke and John, Bless the bed that I lie

on.   Four An-gels to my bed, Two to bot-tom two to head,

Two to hear me when I pray, Two to bear my soul a-way.

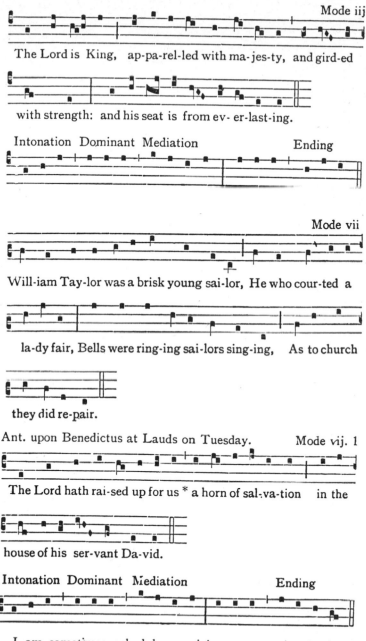

Mode iij

The Lord is King, ap-pa-rel-led with ma-jes-ty, and gird-ed

with strength: and his seat is from ev- er-last-ing.

Intonation Dominant Mediation   Ending

Mode vij

Will-iam Tay-lor was a brisk young sai-lor, He who cour-ted a

la-dy fair, Bells were ring-ing sai-lors sing-ing,   As to church

they did re-pair.

Ant. upon Benedictus at Lauds on Tuesday.   Mode vij. 1

The Lord hath rai-sed up for us * a horn of sal-va-tion   in the

house of his ser-vant Da-vid.

Intonation Dominant Mediation   Ending

I am sometimes asked by musicians unacquainted with the chant to explain certain rather mysterious signs, for instance, at the end of an antiphon there occurs the final notes of the ending of the psalm tone :—

e u o u a e

what do these letter refer to? They are only the vowels of the final words of the "Gloria Patri" or more accurately the end of the second verse beginning "Sicut erat" S/ae/c/u/l/o/rum /A/m/e/n, or in English :—

o i ou e a e

w/o/rld w/i/th/ou/t /e/nd /A/m/e/n.

It is hardly within the scope of this book to give all the nomenclature attached to the plainchant neumes and group of notes, but the entire matter is explained in the Vatican edition of the Roman Gradual, issued by the Plainsong and Mediaeval Music Society (1930).

CHAPTER X

The American Tradition

The American Tradition

AT one time such a title as the above description might have been read with incredulity, not to say amusement when dealing with such a new people given over to every phase of modern life like the Americans. But in recent years through careful study and research, a fresh field of musical interest has been opened out by American musicians; English people, the world over, have been made to realise the very rich store of musical tradition which lies at the foundation of American cultural life today. I can only refer to the work of the late Dr. Pullen Jackson and his quite indispensable range of books in justification for this statement. It is impossible for me to attempt to cover the ground he has so ably surveyed, except in so far as certain forms of musical expression by White and Negro folksingers seem to be carrying out, in recent times, what I contend happened in the earliest ages when the people's jubilations became the responsorial chant of the Church.

Cecil Sharp in his journeys over the Appalachian Mountains found singing populations. Unlike his earlier experience in Somerset and elsewhere in England, his singers were then fairly advanced in life, but the American mountain folk were all a singing people, whatever their age or condition might be. The tradition was therefore more vital in America than in this country.

Furthermore the Religious Revival and the Great Awakening movements in America from the seventeen-forties till well into the nineteenth century, all borrowed from the folk their distinctive and expressive modal melodies in order to bring home to their congregations and assemblies the intense need for a new outlook on life. The leaders of this perfervid desire for conversion did not have to look to catchy tunes, dear to the souls of later nineteenth century missionaries. The music they wanted was ready to hand. They did not adopt music hall emotion to rake souls out of Hellfire corner—the rhythm already in the souls of the folk was sufficient to guide their lives into more amenable spiritual channels when allied, not to the words they had formerly known, but to the new Gospel slogans and scriptural phrases embodied in their metrical hymns. At the period mentioned what we can call English non-Conformity seems to have experienced an amazing emotional expansion in the new found freedom of the United States. No form of ecclesiastical or civil institutionalism could hold back or restrain this sudden outburst, perhaps the result of centuries of suppression in feudal England and the European continent.

Dr. Pullen Jackson points out,* that Cecil Sharp when visiting homes in the Appalachian Mountains rather avoided hearing hymns. Had he listened he might well have heard the folksong element in most of them. I am not surprised at this avoidance, perhaps long experience of hymn singing by respectable English congregations made him fear that valuable time might be wasted if he showed interest in this direction.† However, four years after Sharp's death, Miss A. Gilchrist wrote a most useful article on "The Folk Element in Early Revival Hymns and Tunes."§ This article possessed all the musical knowledge and critical acumen for which Miss Gilchrist has been so well known for many years past. Other American students followed in the same direction and now we have the exhaustive work of Dr. Pullen Jackson. As I have written previously, it is unnecessary to try and supplement what has already been accomplished, but certain features and trends in both White and Negro singing are so striking to a student of the plainchant that he cannot possibly refrain from making a closer examination or even striking a parallel line between ancient and modern practice, and to enquire how far certain aspects, usages and effects in folksinging today may not reflect exactly similar states and conditions in much more remote ages.‡ It is a very delicate matter to attempt to press parallels between the ancient and the modern practices of folksingers, but in the study of folklore, survivals from remote antiquity are for ever present in the customs of people today. Therefore it cannot possibly be urged that any attempt to trace back striking musical effects which appear among modern folksingers is other than relevant to the whole question under investigation.

---

* *Spiritual Folksong of Early America*, Intro. p. 3.
† It may not be out of place to state that Sharp emphasised to me personally the rich fund of music for Church purposes which could be found in his American collections.
§ *J. F. S. S.* No. 32, Vol. VIII, Pt. II, 1928.
‡ I have already made reference to this feature in the chapter dealing with the Romanian signs.

It might be well here to relate personal experiences. We had in this country, and particularly in the county of Norfolk, a Great Awakening or a Great Invasion, not very long ago, by the presence, during several years of the war, of twelve thousand United States soldiers actually in this parish, not to mention very many more thousands on the various airfields in the immediate neighbourhood. American contacts were therefore both varied and numerous, but what my great interest was when I encountered on a nearby gunsight, officers from Virginia and men from the Appalachian Mountains.

At first they seemed a little surprised at my musical enquiries, but realising I knew something about their manners and customs, if only from books, they opened out and I sat for an hour and more while song after song poured out. On one occasion, when enthusiasm rose, the surge or jubilation burst forth and I heard what I was most wanting to hear, the long drawn out notes on the vowel sounds.

However, gunsites were no longer required and my friends departed, but an equally interesting section took their place, five hundred coloured troops. At once reports were prevalent about their vocal capacity, so friendly meetings and interviews quickly followed. They sang in our lovely fifteenth century church here, very different from their home surroundings but I challenge my American friends to find a more suitable environment, in spite of open air assemblies in the genial climate of the Southern States, our high pitched hammer beam roof and the graceful columns made acoustics perfect for the beautiful natural harmonies of the Negro singers.

From a fairly extensive repertoire two spirituals remain in the memory as rather outstanding among a very appealing programme: "Oh Mary, don't you weep," and " There's trouble in the air".

In England it was a unique chance of listening to the "real thing"; the first impression gained from hearing this choir was one of strong emotional appeal, there was pathos and intensity, but at the same time entire spontaneity, real feeling in diction and expression, but of an entirely natural character. The vocalisation showed a full and rich harmonic sense, but the parts seemed in wonderful accord, kept together by the rhythmical genius of the conductor. I fell under the spell of the singing through the subtle hand of the conductor. I pondered over this magic hand on several occasions. The conductor told me that he and his singers could read a musical score, but they sang unaccompanied and

without reference to any printed text. Hence their freedom of
expression and untrammelled technique. Still, the movement of
that hand, far removed from formal conducting, fascinated me.
Preserving the unity of the parts, without apparent effort, his
action showed a sympathy between conductor and singers which
was certainly unusual and I began wondering if the conducting
was not as traditional, both in spirit and action, as the music and
words of the songs. In the remote past, how did the singers keep
together in unison, giving utterance to the long refrains or jubila
tions without words, a living practice both among White as well
as Negro singers, except through the hand of the precentor? The
first beginnings of musical script or characters is called chironomic
notation,* in other words, a written description of the action of
the hand of the leader. Again one of the most moving incidents
in the whole demonstration by this choir was singing or jubilating
with closed lips.

Now these curving grace notes, this surge or jubilation, are
not easy for the trained and educated musician to capture.† The
freedom of expression required under these conditions of spiritual
fervour can only be brought within the notational scope of art
formulae with extreme difficulty. Our ancestors who left these
shores for life in the future United States took their songs with
them, not in song books but in their minds and souls. As life
developed and the colonies expanded so the need for greater
coherence in vocalisation arose. Hence we find an original system
of notation introduced.§ This is response to a particular vocal
need.

Now if my whole contention about the basic unity of folksong and plainsong is correct, do we not see in the ninth century
and up to the thirteenth a very similar process? A process, too,
that showed both knowledge and insight on the part of the precentors or the magistri scholarum, who managed to capture, without the aid of the recording machine, this musical expression from
the soul of the people. Unlike the modern musician with his
trained background derived from centuries of musical technique,
the men and women of the centuries named had been trained,
not in the Conservatoires of Europe or America, but in their own

---

* Vid. Ch. IV, p. 38.

† See Dr. Pullen Jackson's fascinating story *White and Negro Spirituals*,
pp. 246 ff.

§ Art. by Dr. Pullen Jackson in the *Musical Quarterly* "Buckwheat Notes,"
October, 1933, Vol. XIX, No. 4.

domestic circles, where folk customs of song and dance still continued, giving them a true cultural foundation.†

In so far as song and dance vindicate the reality of the human soul, the people of the United States seem to be in a unique position because so many streams of life, such diverse racial currents seek for unity of expression on the American continent. In spite of all political and ethnological divergencies, a true national coherence will arise founded on this sense of rhythm which will remain firm amid every process of modernity. The Negroes certainly possess it in a marked degree, but it is now recognised that the musical tradition enshrined in the spirituals is English rather than African. It still flourishes in the mountain homes of the people and has travelled back in these days to the land of its birth. It was this tradition which was superimposed on the lives and outlook of the Negroes, but the rhythm of it passed through the Negro consciousness and gave expression to their distinctive state and condition, as well as being enhanced by the former characteristics of their history and environment—may we say that, in the case of the Negroes, the "Beat of the Drum" made impact with this English tradition and started a new stream of development.

NOTE I

It is important at the same time to bear in mind very carefully what the Rev. W. H. Melish has written in his recent book "Strength for Struggle" (New York—the Bromwell Press, 1953). Chapter 4 deals with 'Freedom Train,' and shows that the religious sentiments underlying the "Spirituels" did not arise from a feeling of "otherworldliness," but were definitely concerned with the actual state and condition of the "here and now".

Hence the verse :—

> Glory to God and Jesus too,
> One more soul is safe!
> Oh, go and carry the news
> One more soul got safe . . .

actually refers to the suspension bridge in Canada over which negro slaves gained their freedom. The Spirituels have the nature of revolutionary slogans like the 14th century peasants cry in England.

---

† I feel I must record my complete agreement with and thanks to the author, already named, throughout his Ch. XVIII, *The Country Singing Manner. The Surge Song Secret is Out.*

When Adam delved and Eve span,
Who was then the gentleman?

Rev. W. H. Melish adds (p. 42) "Negro spirituels were born out of this struggle, they are not religious escapism at all but a direct reflection of the Negroes aspiration for a better life in this present world."

NOTE II

Those who have studied the Introduction to Sharp's first issue of "English Folk Songs from the Southern Appalachians" (G. P. Putnam's Sons 1917) will be interested in the following statement by Miss Maud Karpeles which appeared in the Bulletin of the International Folk Music Council, 1951.

"The purpose of my mountain excursion was to follow up my footsteps of thirty years ago, when I had collected folksongs of English origin with the late Cecil Sharp. Then, there were few roads through the mountains and the people were living self-contained lives almost completely shut off from the rest of the world. Cecil Sharp and I spent fifty weeks in the mountains and during that time we never heard a bad tune; if anyone sang at all it was a folk song. Now, roads and electricity have brought "civilisation" into the mountains. The roads have made markets accessible and the people are busy earning a living, but there is less time to enjoy life. Electricity has brought the radio, and "hilly-billy" can be heard at any time of the day, but genuine folk songs which were previously so plentiful must now be patiently sought. With most of the singers, memory has weakened, but the love of the old songs still lies dormant and it requires only a little encouragement for it to spring up anew. It was a great delight to many a singer to be able to re-learn a forgotten song from the printed version made from his singing of thirty years ago. Thus, a song originating in England is carried orally to America and develops there; after, perhaps, a couple of hundred years it is brought back to England in written form; thirty years later the published song is carried back to the country of its adoption and again it takes on a new lease of life. Through such vicissitudes does tradition persist."

CHAPTER XI

American Tradition
(Continued)

"The Beat of the Drum"

American Tradition

(Continued)

"The Beat of the Drum"

THE above sentence calls forth a further emotion and therefore description. The jubilation, the surge, the sound (soni) are beyond words, but there comes a moment when the human voice cannot restrain the energy, the exertion which wells out in even greater activity. The ancient ballad is a particular instance of this feeling. The tribal group could not remain still while the story continued, they must all participate and so the movement of the dance arose. It was the expression of the entire personality, the music of the limbs. Dancing is therefore a very sensitive form of human feeling. The folk dance, the world over, is both primaeval and modern because it enshrines what is eternal, overmastering, in natural emotion.

Now the rhythmical quality which calls forth the folksong is equally or perhaps more apparent in the folk dance. Both forms of rhythm appear as living traditions in the United States.* Now it may seem strange that such a country with so strong a Puritan foundation should have wanted to preserve folk customs so powerfully tinged with the pagan element surrounding anything connected with fertility worship. The Puritans in this country, once in power, quickly dealt with the maypoles because they considered undesirable sexual practices followed from the maypole dances. But the now rather famous Playford's Dancing Master appeared during the Commonwealth period (1650). Whatever

---

* Douglas and Helen Kennedy: *Square Dances of America,* also C. J. Sharp and M. Karpeles: *The Running Set,* Novello.

official Puritanism may have done to curb or control human impulse, they seem to have had little permanent success even in the land where their opportunities might appear to be greatest for successfully exercising a policy of suppression.

While sharing the simplicity and some of the rigidity of the Puritans, the Society of Friends, the Quakers, were fundamentally different from the former in their whole teaching and approach to the nature of mankind.* About 1747, two Quakers, Jane and James Wardley, became infected with teaching which looked upon the second advent of Christ as practically immediate. A certain Ann Lee from Manchester was drawn towards this particular group of Quakers, "Shaking Quakers" as they came to be called. It is well to emphasise the fervently apocalyptic character of their message because, after passing through considerable physical persecution and intense spiritual experiences, she, with other members of the Society, landed in America in 1774. This was the commencement of the Shaker Movement in the United States. My reason for selecting this particular sect or group, amongst all the other varieties of religious experience in the States, is that their worship, ceremonial, social and spiritual teaching centred round a definite system of song and dance. The soul of man is expressed through rhythm, and rhythm is the soul of the dance, whether rendered vocally or by movement of the limbs. It was certainly a right joyous way of anticipating the second Advent. However, the rhythm they wanted was ready to hand in both song and dance because the "Shakers" were imbued with the spirit of a true folk art.† Furthermore the "Shakers" claimed divine sanction, not to say direct revelation, for their dance movements although the choreographical descriptions in the book by Mr. Edward D. Andrews would be fairly familiar to any folk dancer and must have made alignment with the general dancing customs of the people at this period, 1774-1840 onwards. However, the psychological background of the whole matter is very interesting because the "Shakers" were no Puritans. Yet they strove for simplicity and

---

* Vid. Robert Barclay: *An Apology for True Christian Divinity,* a treatise addressed to Charles II, 1675.

† Vid. Edward D. Andrews: *The Gift to be Simple,* J. J. Augustin, New York. I am deeply grateful to the author of this most fascinating book who has detected, explained and made abundantly clear the underlying significance of this extraordinary phase in American religious life and therefore its contribution to American culture. I would call particular attention to the illustrations of the Shaker ceremonial dance. Those of us who are familiar with the balance and poise required in the folk dance would recognise from these illustrations this distinctive attitude of the folk dancer.

a distinctive form of asceticism as witnessed in their celibate lives.
To them sexuality was the devil,* but the said devil must be openly
faced and overcome and their method for acquiring self-control
was the sublimation found in the movements of the dance. Far
from promoting promiscuous sexuality the "Shakers" felt that the
intricacies to be found in the patterns of their dances avoided
rather than aggravated physical impulse and therefore the rhythm
of the soul could overcome any too obvious physical sensation,
which might rise from contacts during the dance movements. I
feel I must quote the following from Mr. Andrews' book *Gift to
be Simple,* p. 12, because it is so indicative of much earlier
practice,† in other words twist the devil's tail by purloining his
music, hence :

> "Let justice seize old Adam's crew,
> And all the whore's production;
> We'll take the choicest of their songs,
> Which to the Church of God belongs,
> And recompense them for their wrongs,
> In singing their destruction."

Dr. Pullen Jackson comments in the same book,§ on the intangible
character of the folk method in singing which was certainly evident
among the Shaker Communities, who invented their own form
of notation and also a choreography drawn from their folk inheritance more than from any formal composition.

To sum up the whole matter in relation to the United States
cultural traditions; when a nation or a group of nations is becoming culturally articulate, and external circumstances seem to create
a spiritual and physical crisis in life generally human emotion must
find both an outlet and a satisfaction. The rhythm of music seems
to supply this need and meet the required reaction. Surely this
was the case in the fourth and again in the ninth century? America
was in a surprisingly similar situation from the Day of Independ-
ence to the Civil War. The various racial streams, the human
impacts, the desire to expand and the sense of adventure with
all the very varied religious currents combined to demand

---

* op. cit. p. 17.

> "I mean to be obedient,
> And cross my ugly nature,
> And share the blessings that are sent
> To ev'ry honest creature,
> With ev'ry gift I will unite
> And join in sweet devotion:
> To worship God is my delight
> With hands and feet in motion."

† Vid. Clement of Alexandria already quoted p. 3.

§ *Gift to be Simple,* p. 90.

emotional satsfaction in the only manner and method that was really possible. The folk from the British Isles, now Americans, reacted in the human and therefore right direction by turning to the basic expression found in their own souls, the rhythm of their songs and dances.

In conclusion, and by way of contrast, let us turn to old Europe to the land of enduring traditions, to the country of the Basques, to Southern France and Northern Spain, to the vision of the lofty Pyrenees looking down on the unchanging emotional life of humanity.* Here in spite of all apparent changes, Moorish incursions, Catholic culture and the incidence of revolutionary ideas, the psychology of a people seems to have been settled and fixed around the basic impulses which are eternal in human existence. The songs, dances and the folk drama of these people clearly contain elements which are at once both primaeval and modern, hence, if it is not a misnomer, we have a living folklore.†

I do not mean that Catholicism has not made a transposition or a transformation, I have myself witnessed Spanish peasants, with awe and reverence, but with all the characteristics of folk ceremonial, dance round a statue of our Lady of Lourdes. The action and the underlying principle is the same and even when the motive is exalted, the human desire for procreation must be met. With Catholic ideology this natural yearning does not look so much to the process of sexual relations as to the ultimate result and fruition in the childbearing. The late Mr. G. K. Chesterton has a very illuminating passage in one of his early essays,§ how prehistoric man when thinking of the central unit of life in the family, would place the social order of precedence in the father, mother, child. But the Christian Revolution lay in the complete reversal of this principle which henceforward must be read, child, mother, father, and this the Catholic Church calls not the family but the "Holy Family". Mr. Chesterton adding: "Because many things are made holy by being turned upside down."

---

* Vid. Two very useful books—Violet Alford: *Pyrenean Festivals*, and Rodney Gallop: *The Book of the Basques*. At Cecil Sharp House and at the Albert Hall on several occasions we have been enabled to witness teams of dancers from all the districts named in the text, so what is described does represent a certain actual knowledge and experience of the music and dancing of these people.

† Violet Alford: *Pyrenean Festivals*, op. cit. p. 231, ff. Miss Alford here refers to the parallel instincts which gave rise to the primaeval wall paintings at Cogul and the attitude in song and dance of Pyrenean womenfolk today.

§ G. K. Chesterton: *Heretics*, p. 179, John Lane and Co.

So whether we view the New World or the Old World, whatever changes take place in knowledge, circumstances or environment, the emotional pattern of our lives is always the same and the safest channels for self-expression have been found through the ages to be development and appreciation of that inner quality we call rhythm, which is at once the guide and safeguard when faced with the wayward tendencies of the natural man.

CHAPTER XII

Suggestions for Further Study and Research

Suggestions for Further Study
and Research

It is only possible to give a brief summary because the range of study can be very wide. On the one side there is a vast extent of literature on the plainchant, largely centring round the research and work of the monastery at Solesmes : there the monks have been actively engaged in the examination and collation of MSS for more than half a century. On the other side, there is the whole study of folklore in its several interesting channels and aspects; as is fairly well known this movement is not confined to one nation but has a European or international interest. It may be advisable to give the chief authorities with a view to promoting further and perhaps more intensive investigation.

S. Augustine's Commentary on the Psalms—"Patrologia Latina ed. Migne, Paleographie Musicale (Solesmes)." "The Winchester Troper", ed. Henry Bradshaw Society with introduction by the late Dr. Frere. This introduction, and the authorities cited, are quite indispensable for the purpose in hand. The Facsimile copies of the Sarum Gradual and Antiphonary (Plainsong and Medieval Music Society).

The other publications of the Plainsong and Medieval Music Society are carefully selected by skilled musicians and represent a neat transference of the plainsong to the English text. Here the work of the late Drs. Palmer and Frere are outstanding, the former has rendered the Sarum breviary with the full musical text into English.* It is difficult adequately to apprize Dr. Palmer's work in this direction, his musical and liturgical knowledge were profound, and towards the end of his life his interest in the folk music increased, on one occasion, I remember, his friend the late Dr. Woodward, handing him some Scotch traditional folk melodies,

---

* Vid Convent of S. Mary, Wantage, publishers.

which promptly brought from him the illuminating remark : "I know several antiphons reflecting that theme." Reference has already been made to his translations of the ancient hymns : further renderings will be found in "The Hymner"* and mention must also be made of his *"English Plainchant Psalter"*.

The very important work rendered by the Anglican Gregorian Association must also be emphasised. The former Director of this organisation, the late Rev. Francis Burgess, rendered very valuable service to the cause of the chant and the polyphonic music. He issued through the Plainchant Publications Committee (6 Hyde Park Gate, London, S.W.7) many useful choir books which have had a helpful influence in several places. These works show both the width of knowledge and the musical insight of the editor.

Of text books the most important is the late Professor Wagner's *Introduction to the Gregorian Melodies,* Pt. I, translated by Agnes Orme and E. G. P. Wyatt.†

Gregorian Music, and *A Grammar of Plainsong,* by the Benedictines of Stanbrook, Worcester.

Church Music Monograph Series,§ *Plainchant,* by Dom Gatard, O.S.B., and *Byzantine Music* by Professor Tillyard.

The student of rhythm should also consult the life of Richard Rolle of Hampole, together with his *English Lyrics* by F. M. M. Comper,‡ also by the same editor, R. Rolle's *Fire of Love,* or *Melody of Love,* etc.** Then there is the passage from the *Summa* of S. Thomas Aquinas referred to in the treatise which represents the psychological side of the subject, and also the two sets of lectures by the late Dr. Rudolf Steiner on *Eurhythmy as Visible Speech* and *Eurhythmy as Visible Song.*†† On this very intricate study these two works ought not to be passed over.

Important articles are found in the *Catholic Encyclopaedia* and in the *Jewish Encyclopaedia.* On folksongs there are now numerous editors and publications. The library at Cecil Sharp House contains the most important collections. The Sharp MSS are at Clare College, Cambridge, and, let us hope, in due time will receive the exhaustive study and collation with other MSS which this collection fully deserves. The Journals of the former English Folksong Society (now joined to the Folk Dance Society)

---

* Plainsong and Medieval Music Society.
† Plainsong and Medieval Music Society.
§ Faith Press Limited.
‡ J. M. Dent & Sons Limited.
** Methuen Limited.
†† Steiner Library, 35 Park Road, London, N.W.1.

are essential to any thorough investigation of the subject. Quite recently (1954) a "Guide to English Folk Song Collections" has been written by Margaret Dean-Smith (University of Liverpool and E.F.D.S.S.).

Mention must also be made of the wider experience of Miss Violet Alford and Mr. Rodney Gallop, who, from the angle of the dance, have written some most useful works showing both exceptional knowledge and critical insight of the whole subject.*

A collection has been made from the papers on liturgical subjects by the late Dr. Frere. The essay on *The Palaeography of Early Mediaeval Music* (pg. 90) in this volume deserves very careful study.†

In 1941 Gustav Reese's work *Music in the Middle Ages* first appeared in this country. To emphasise and then pass over the value of this book would be unjust to an able and exact scholar. The content, arrangement and pattern of this volume is of first rate importance and it was his reference to S. John Chrysostom which enabled me to expand my chapter on the Patristic testimony in relation to the chant. As I have already suggested, the advance in recent years in musical research in the United States has been truly extensive. The labours and publications of Dr. George Pullen Jackson are outstanding. Besides the books already referred to there is a further considerable range of his works in the library at Cecil Sharp House, published by J. J. Augustin, New York. Mention must again be made of that delightfully interesting book by Edward G. Andrews *The Gift to be Simple*.§ It is scarcely necessary to point out that the above references and recommendations hardly touch the fringe of the subject.

Looking back over the years when, as a choirboy I first heard a Gregorian chant, down to the middle nineties when Vespers at Solesmes became the "Poetry of Europe", and then on to the issue of the "Motu Proprio" of his Holiness St. Pius X, plainsong became a life interest only to be enhanced when in 1910 I first heard the "White Pater Noster" in its familiar Phrygian mode. Much water has flowed down the stream since then and it has been hardly possible to keep track of everything one has read and studied, or to mention the many friends and authors to whom I am greatly indebted. Finally articles appear in *Music and Letters* and the *American Musical Quarterly* which are invaluable not only for their content but also for keeping knowledge and interest up to date.

---

* Violet Alford and Rodney Gallop: *The Traditional Dance*, Methuen. Violet Alford: *English Folk Dances*. Rodney Gallop: *A Book on the Basques*.
† Oxford University Press.   § J. J. Augustin, New York.

APPENDIX

Clement of Alexandria

Paedagogus Lib. II, Ch. IV, p. 439 ff. Tom VIII Patr. Lat.

"Quomodo conviviis se recreare oportet."

"Sunt enim admittendae moderatae et pudicae harmoniae : contra a forti et nervosa nostra mente vere molles harmoniae amandandae quam longissime, quae improbo flexuum vocis artificio ad effeminatam mollitium et scurrilitatem deducunt. Graves autem, et pudicae modulationes ebrietatis proterviae nuntium remittunt. Chromaticae harmoniae, impudenti in vino proterviae floribusque redimitae et meretriciae musicae sunt relinquendae.

*   *   *   *

Ut supra—Graecum Textum :

Καὶ γὰρ ἁρμονίας παραδεκτέον τὰς σώφρονας· ἀπωτάτω ὅτι μάλιστα ἐλαύνοντας τῆς ἐρρωμένης ἡμῶν διανοίας, τας ὑλρὰς ὄντως ἁρμονίας, αἵ περὶ τὰς καμπὰς των φθόλλων κακοτεχνοῦσαι εἰς θρύψιν και βωμολοχίαν ἐκδιαιτῶνται· τὰ δὲ αὐστηρὰ καὶ σωφρονικὰ μέλη ἀποτάσσεται ταῖς τῆς μέθης ἀλερωχίαις. Καταλειπτέον οὖν τὰς χρωματικὰς ἁρμονίας ταῖς ἀχρώμοις παροινίαις καὶ τῇ ἀνθοφορούσῃ καὶ ἑταιρουσῃ μουσικῇ.

S. Augustine

Enarr. in ps. XXXII, 1 - 8

Ecce veluti modum cantandi dat tibi : noli quaerere verba quasi explicare possis unde Deus oblectetur : ' In jubilatione cane . . . quid est in jubilatione canere? Intelligere verbis explicare non posse quod canitur corde. Etenim ille qui cantant sive in messe sive in vinea, sive in aliquo opere ferventi, cum coeperint in verbis canticorum exultare laetitia, veluti impleti tanta laetitia ut eam verbis explicare non possint, avertunt se a syllabis verborum et eunt in sonum jubilationis. Jubilus sonus quidem est significans cor parturire quod dicere non potent.

Enarr. in ps. XCIX, 4.

Qui jubilat, non verba dicit sed sonus quidem est laetitiae sine verbis. . . . Gaudens homo in exultatione sua ex verbis quibusdam quae non possunt dici et intelligi erumpit in vocem quamquam exultationis sine verbis : ita ut appareat cum ipsa voce gaudere quidem, sed quasi repletum nimis gaudio non posse verbis explicare quod gaudet.

Enarr, ps. XCVII

"Jubilate Deo universa terra." Jam nostis quid sit jubilare. Gaudete et loquamini. Si quod gaudetis loqui non potestis, jubilate : gaudium vestrum exprimat jubilatio, si non potest locutio : non sit tamen mutum gaudium.

Ibid. ps. XLVI

"Ascendit Deus in jubilatione." Quid est jubilatio, nisi admiratio gaudii quae verbis non potest explicari.

Ibid. ps. XLIV

Quid est jubilare? Gaudium verbis non posse explicari, et tamen voce testari quod intus conceptum est, et verbis explicari non potest, hoc est jubilare. Nam considerat charitas vestra qui jubilant in cantilenis quibusque, et quasi in certamine quodam laetitae saecularis et vidistis quasi inter cantica verbis expressa exundantes laetitia, cui lingua dicendo non sufficit, quemadmodum jubilent, ut per illam vocem indicetur animi affectus verbis explicari non valuistis quod corde concipitur. Si ergo illi de gaudio terreno jubilant, nos de gaudio caelesti jubilare non debemus, quod vere verbis explicari non possumus?

Ch. VII Libr. IX *Confessiones*. ibid.

Tunc hymni et psalmi ut canerentur secundum morem orientalium partium ne populus moeroris taedio contabesceret, institutum est; et ex illo in hodiernum retentum, multis jam ac pene omnibus gregibus tuis et per caetera orbis imitantibus.

* * * *

S. Isidore of Seville

Vol. 32, p. 164, *De Musica* 132, Ch. XV Etymol. Lib. III.
Patr. Migne.

Ch. XVII

1. Itaquae sine musica nulla disciplina potest esse perfecta, nihil enim est sine illa. Nam et ipsi mundus quadam harmonia sonorum fertur esse compositus, et caelum sub harmonia modulatione revolvitur. Musica movit affectus, provocat in diversum habitum sensus.

2. In praeliis quoque tubae concentus pugnantes accendit : et quanto vehementior fuerit clangor, tanto fit fortior ad certamen animus.

Siquidem et remigiis cantus hortatur.

Ad tolerandos quoque labores musica animum mulcet, et singulorum operum fatigationem modulatio vocis solatur.

Ch. 20, sec. 2

Harmonia est modulatio vocis et concordantia plurimorum sonorum vel coaptatio.

136 : 8 Cantus est inflexio vocis, nam sonus directus est, praecedit autem sonus cantum.

136 : 9 Arsis est vocis elevatio, id est initium, thesis vocis positio, hoc est finis.

S. Hilary

Comment on Ps. LXV (Vers. 2 and 3) "Jubilate Deo"
(Patr. Migne p. 425)

3. Jubilum quid vulgo secundum vim vocis graecae sonus est militaris. In latinis codicibus ita legimus : jubilate Deo omnis terra. Et quantum ad eloquii nostri consuetudinem pertinet, jubilum pastoralis agrestisque vocis sonum nuncupamus, cum in solitudinibus aut respondens aut requirens, per significantium ductae in longum et expressae in nisum sonus vocis auditur. In graecis vero libris, qui ex hebraeo proximi sunt, non eadem significantia scribitur. Namque ita se habent : ἀλαλάζατε τῷ Θεῷ πασα ἡ γῇ et cum illis ἀλαλαγμὸς quem latine jubilum ponunt, significat vocem exercitus praeliantis, aut in concursu proterentis hostem aut successum victoriae exsultationis voce testantis. Quam rem ubi ita se translationis ratio temperavit absolutius in psalmo altero

intelligimus cum dicit : omnes gentes plaudite manibus jubilate Deo in voce exsultationis.

Ps. 46. 2. Vix autem exsultationis dissentit ab jubilo; sed pro translationis conditione quia propria exsultantis vocis nuncupatio non reperta est, per id quod jubilum dicitur, vox exsultantis ostenditur.

Decree X of the Council of Cloveshoo shows the desire to instruct the clergy in the meaning and significance of their office and if ignorant of the sense of the words of the Mass and Baptism they must learn. (Vid. Mansi-Amplissima Collecta concilia, XII, 1901, 399.)

Decree XII

Duodecimo adjunxerunt edicto, ut presbyteri saecularium poetarum modo in ecclesia non garriant, ne tragico sono sacrorum verborum compositionem ac distinctionem corrumpant vel confundant, sed simplicem sanctamque melodiam secundum morem ecclesiae sectentur : quivero id non est idoneus assequi pronunciantis modo simpliciter legendo, dicat atque recitet quidquid instantis temporis ratio possit; et qui episcopi sunt non praesumant.

Decree XIII

Tertio definitur decreto, ut uno codemque modo dominicae dispensationis in carne sacrosanctae festivitatis, in omnibus ad eas rite competentibus rebus, id est in baptismi officio, in missarum celebratione, in cantilenae modo celebrentur juxta exemplar videlicet quod scriptum de Romana habemus ecclesia.

Decree XV

Quinto-decimo definierunt capitulo, ut septem canonicae orationum diei et noctis horae diligente cura cum psalmodia et cantilena sibimet convenienti observentur, et ut eamdem monasterialis psalmodiae parilitatem ubique sectentur, nihilque quod communis usus non admittit, praesumant cantare aut legere, sed tantum quod ex sacrarum scripturarum auctoritate descendit, et quod Romanae ecclesiae consuetudo permittit, cantent vel legant, quatenus unanimi uno re laudent Deum. . . .

*   *   *   *

S. Isidore

De Musica 132. Ch. XV, Etym. Lib. III, Migne Patr. Vol. 82

1. Musica est peritia modulationis sono cantuque consistens : et dicta musica per derivationem a Musis. Musae autem appellatae, ἀπὸ τοῦ μῶσθαι, id est a qaerendo, quod per eas sicut antiqui voluerunt vis carminum et vocis modulatio quaereretur.

2. Quarum sonus quia sensibilis res est praeterfluit in praeteritum tempus imprimitur memoriae, inde a poetis Jovis et memoriae filias Musas esse confectum est. Nisi enim ab homine memoria teneantur soni, pereant quia scribi non possunt.

*   *   *   *

S. Aldhelm

William of Malmesbury — Gesta Pontificum — Rolls Series, 1870,
ed. N.E.S.A. Hamilton, pp. 336, 190, Lib. V.

Litteris itaque ad plenum instructus, nativae quoque linguae non negligebat carmina; adeo teste libro Elfredi de quo superius dixi, nulla unquam aetate par ei fuerit quisquam. Poesim Anglicam posse facere, cantum componere, eadem apposite vel canere vel dicere. Denique commemorat Elfredus carmen trivale, quod adhuc vulgo cantitatur. Adelmum fecisse, bis quae videantur frivola institisse. Populum eo tempore semibarbarium, parum divinis sermonibus intentum, statim cantatis missis, domos cursitare solitum. Ideo sanctum virum, super pontem qui rura et urbem continuat, abeuntibus se apposuisse obicem, quasi artem cantitando professim. Eo plusquam semel facto, plebis favorem et concursum emeritum. Hoc commento sensim inter ludicra verbis scripturarum insertis, cives ad sanitatem reduxisse : qui ei severe et cum excommunicatione agendum putasset profecto profecisset nichil.

*   *   *   *

'*Summa*' of *S. Thomas Aquinas*

Secunda Secundae Quest: CLXXX — Art. VI

. . .Operatio intellectus, in qua contemplatio essentialiter consistit, motus dicitur, secundum quod motus est actus perfecti, ut Philosophus dicit (De anima lib III, text 28). Quia vero per sensibilia in cognitionem intelligibilium devenimus operationes autem sensibiles sine motu non fiunt : vide est quod etiam operationes intelligibiles quasi motus quidam describuntur, et secundum similitudinem diversorum motuum earum differentia assignatur. In motibus autem corporalibus perfectiores et primi sunt locales ut probatur. (Phys. Lib. VIII, text 55 et 57). Et ideo sub corum similitudine potissimae operationes intelligibiles describuntur. Quorum quidem sunt tres differentiae : nam quidam est circularis secundum quem aliquid movetur uniformiter circa idem centrum : alius autem est rectus, secundum quem aliquid procedit ab uno circulars carens principio et fine, uniformiter est circa idem in aluid; tertius autem est obliquus quasi compositus ex utroque.

"Ad secundum dicendum". . . . ff. Et ideo Dionysius motum circularem in angelis assignat inquantum uniformiter et indesinenter absque principio et fine intuentur Deum; sicut motus circularis cantens principio et fine, uniformiter est circa idem centrum. In anima vero, antequam ad istam uniformitatem perveniat, exigitur quod duplex ejus difformitas amoveatur.

Gerbert : *De Cantu et Musica Sacra* — A.D. 1754.
Lib. I. Cantus Prim. Eccles. Aet.· p. 198.
"Harmonica" (juxta Cassiodorum) scientia est musica, quae discernit in sonis acutum et grave.
"Rhythmica," quae requirit in concursione verborum, utrum bene fons vel male cohaereat.
"Metrica" est, quae mensuras diversonum metrorum probabili ratione cognoscit; ut verbi gratia, "heroicum", "iambicum", "elegiacum", et caetera.

*   *   *   *

S. Joannis Chrys:

In Ps. 41. Migne Patr. Graeco-Latina, Vol. LV, pp. 155/6

Μᾶλλον δὲ ἀναγκαῖον εἰπεῖν πρῶτον, τίνος ἕνεκεν ὁ ψαλμὸς εἰς τὸν βίον εἰσενήκεται τὸν ἡμέτερον, καὶ μετ' ᾠδῆς μάλιστα αὕτη ἡ προφετεία λέγεται. Τίνος οὖν ἕνεκεν λέγεται μετ' ᾠδῆς, ἄκουσον· πολλοὺς τῶν ἀνθρώπων κατιδὼν ὁ Θεὸς ῥαθυμοτέρους ὄντας, καὶ πρὸς τὴν τῶν πνευματικῶν ἀνάγνωσιν δυσχερῶς ἔχοντας, καὶ τὸν ἐκεῖθεν οὐχ ἡδέως ὑπομένοντας κάματον, ποθεινότερον ποιῆσαι τόν πόνον βουλόμενος, καὶ τοῦ καμάτου τήν αἴσθησιν ὑποτεμέσθαι, μελῳδίαν ἀνέμιξε τῇ προφητείᾳ, ἵνα τῷ ῥυθμῷ τοῦ μέλους ψυχαλωλούμενοι πάντες, μετὰ πολλῆς τῆς προθυμίας τοὺς ἀναπέμπωσιν αὐτῷ ὕμνους. Οὐδὲν γὰρ οὐδὲν οὕτως ἀνίστησι ψυχήν, καὶ πτεροῖ, καὶ τῆς γῆς ἀπαλλάττει, καὶ τῶν τοῦ σώματος ἀπολύει δεσμῶν, καὶ φιλοσοφεῖν ποιεῖ, καὶ πάντων καταγελᾶν τῶν βιωτικῶν, ὡς μέλος συμφωνίας, καὶ ῥυθμῷ συγκείμενον θεῖον ᾆσμα· οὕτω γοῦν ἡμῶν ἡ φύσις πρὸς τὰ ᾄσματα καὶ τὰ μέλη ἡδέως ἔχει καὶ οἰκείως, ὡς καὶ τὰ ὑπομάζια παιδία κλαυθμυριζόμενα καὶ δυσχεραίνοντα, οὕτω κατακοιμίζεσθαι. Αἱ γοῦν τίτθαι ἐν ταῖς ἀλκάλαις ἀντὰ βαστάζουσαι, πολλάκις ἀπιοῦσαί τε καὶ ἐπανιοῦσαι, καὶ τινα αὐτοῖς κατεπᾴ δουσαι, ᾄσματα παιδικὰ, οὕτως ἀντῶν τὰ βλέφαρα κατακοιμίζουσι. Διὰ τοῦτο καὶ ὁδοιπόροι πολλάκις κατακοιμίζουσι. Διὰ τοῦτο καὶ ὁδοιπόροι πολλάκις κατὰ μεσημβρίαν ἐλαύνοντες ὑποζύγια ᾄδοντεα τοῦτο ποιοῦσαι, τὴν ἐκ τῆς ὁδοιποφίας ταλαιπωίαν ταῖς ᾠδαῖς ἐκείναις παραμυθούμενοι. Οὐχ ὁδοιπόροι δὲ μόνον, ἀλλὰ καὶ γηπόνοι ληνοσατοῦντες, καὶ τρογῶντες, καὶ ἀμπέλους θεραπεύοντεα, καὶ ἄλλο ὁτιοῦν ἐργαζόμενοι, πολλάκις ᾄδουσι· Καὶ ναῦται κωπηλατοῦντες τοῦτο ποιοῦσιν. Ἤδη δὲ καὶ γυναῖκες ἱστουργοῦσαι, καὶ τῇ κερκίδι τοὺς στήμονας συγκεχυμένους διακρίνουσαι, πολλάκια μὲν καὶ καθ' 'ἑαυτὴν ἑκάστη, πολλάκις σὲ καὶ συμφώνως ἅπασαι, μίαν τινὰ μελῳδίαν ᾄδουσι. Ποιοῦσι δέ τοῦτο καὶ γυναῖκες, καὶ ὁδοιπόροι, καὶ γηπόνοι καὶ ναῦται, τῷ ᾄσματι τον ἐκ των ἔργων πόνον παραμνθή σασθαι σπένδοντες, ὡς τῆς φυχῆς, εἰ μέλους ἀκούσειε καὶ ᾠδῆς ῥᾶον ἅπαντα ἐνεγκεῖν δυναμένης τα ὀχληρὰ καὶ ἐπίπονα. Ἐπεὶ οὖν οἰκείως ἡμῖν πρὸς τουτο ἔχει τὸ εἶδος τῆς τερψεως ἡ ψυχή, ἵνα μὴ πορνικὰ ᾄσματα οἱ δαίμονες εἰσάγοντες, ἅπαντα ἀνατρέπωσι, τοὺς ψαλμοὺς ἐπετείχισεν ὁ Θεός, ὥστε ὁμοῦ καὶ ἡδονὴν το πρᾶγμα καὶ ὠφέλειαν ἐνᾶι. Ἀπὸ μὲν γὰρ τῶν ἔξωθεν ᾀσμάτων βλάβη, καὶ ὄλεθρος, καὶ πολλὰ ἂν εἰσαχθείη δεινά· τὰ γὰρ ἀσελγέστερα καὶ παρανομώτερα τῶν ᾀσμάτων τούτων τοῖς τῆς ψυχῆς μέρεσιν ἐγγινόμενα, ἀσθενεστέραν αὐτὴν καὶ μαλακωτέραν ποιοῦσιν· ἀπὸ δὲ τῶν ψαλμῶν τῶν πνευματικῶν πολυμεν το κέρδος, πολλὴ δὲ ἡ ὠφέλεια, πολυς δὲ ὁ ἁγιασμὸς καὶ πάσης φιλοσοφίας ὑπόθεσις γένοιτ' ἂν τῶν τε ῥημάτων τὴν ψυχὴν ἐκκαθαιρόντων, τοῦ τε ἁγίου Πνεύματος τῇ τὰ τοιαῦτα ψαλλούσῃ ταχέως ἐφιπταμένου ψυχῇ. Ὅτι γὰρ οἱ μετὰ συνέσεως ψάλλοντες τὴν τοῦ πνεύματος καλοῦσι χάριν, ἄκουσον τί φησιν ὁ παῦλος. Μή μεθύσκεσθε οἴνῳ, ἐν ᾧ, ἐστιν ἀσωτία ἀλλὰ πληροῦσθε ἐν Πνευματι ᾽Επήγαγε δὲ καὶ τόν τρόπον τῆς πληρώσεως.

῎Αδοντες καὶ ψάλλοντες ἐν ταῖς καρδίαις ὑμῶν τῳ Κυρίῳ· τί ἐστιν. ᾽Εν ταῖς καρδίαις ὑμῶν; Μετὰ συνέσεως φησίν· ἵναμὴ τὸ στόμα μὲνλαλῇ τὰ ῥήματα, ἡ διάνοια δὲ διατρίβῃ πανταχοῦ πλανωμένη· ἀλλ᾽ἵνα ἀκούη ἡ ψυχὴ τῆς γλώττης.

Β΄

Καὶ καθάπερ ἔνθα μὲν βόρβορος, χοῖροι τρέχουσιν· ἔνθα δὲ ἀρώματα καὶ θυμιάματα μέλιτται κατασκηνουσιν· οὕτως ἔνθα μὲν ᾄσματα πορνικὰ δαίμονες ἐπισωρεύονται· ἔθα δεμέλη πνευματικὰ ἡ τοῦ Πνευματος ἐφίπταται χάρις, καὶ τὸ στόμα καὶ τὴν ψυχὴν ἁγιάζει. Ταῦτα λέγω οὐχ ἵνα ἐπαινῆτε μόνον, ἀλλ᾽ἵνα καὶ παῖδας καὶ γυαῖκας τὰ τοιᾶντα διδάσκητε ᾄσματα ᾄδειν, οὐκ ἐν ἱστοῖς μόνον, οὐδὲ ἐν τοῖς ἄλλοις ἔργοις ἀλλὰ μαλιστα ἐν τραπέζῃ. ᾽Επειδη γὰρ ὡς τὰ πολλὰ ἐν συμποσίοις ὁ διάβολος ἐφεδρεύει μεθην καὶ ἀδηφαγίαν ἔχων αὐτῷ συμμαχοῦσαν, καὶ γέλωτα ἄτακτου καὶ ψυχὴν ἀνειμένην, μαλιστα τότε δεῖ καὶ πρὸ τραπέζης, ἐπιτειχίζειν αὐτῷ τὴν ἀποτῶν ψαλμῶν ἀσφάλειαν, καὶ κοινῇ μετὰ τῆς γυναικὸς καὶ τῶν παίδων ἀναστάντας ἀπὸ τοῦ συμποσίου τους ἱερούς ᾄδειν ὕμνους τῷ Θεῷ.

Early lives of Charlemagne, Ed. A. J. Grant. King's Classics Series, 1905. Reference to Jaffé's Bibliotheca Rerum Germanicarum and Pertz—Monumenta Germaniac Historica. These texts differ in some respects but in this particular passage—Book I. 19—are the same.

"Shortly after a young man, a relation of the emperor, sang on the occasion of some festival the Alleluia admirably, and the Emperor turned to this same bishop and said: "My clerk is singing very well." But the stupid man thought that he was jesting and did not know the clerk was the Emperor's relation and so he answered: "Every peasant can sing as easily to the oxen while he is ploughing."

Latin—Sic omnes pellilparii possunt bubuo agricolantibus vetrenere. Pertz inserts the following note:—

"So kann jeder Bauer seinen Ochsen am Pfluge was vordrönen." "Vetrenere" corresponds to the two words "langide canere"—to sing without effort.

INDEX

Obituary

Fr George died in March 1969 at the age of 88. He was one of the pioneers in the revival of the English Folk Dances and Songs. As a young man he was drawn to the religious life and became a novitiate in the Anglican Community at Caldey in South Wales, but after a few years he left to assist Fr Conrad Noel in his recent appointment as vicar of Thaxted.

It was in 1911 that Conrad and Miriam Noel introduced the newly revived Folk Dancing into Thaxted as a recreation for the younger people in this rather remote corner of Essex. Fr George took an active part in this and Folk Dancing became one of his life's enthusiasms. The leading person in the revival at this time was Mary Neal and it was her version which was taught and flourished at Thaxted until the outbreak of the first world war in which so many of the splendid Thaxted dancers were killed. After the war, when Cecil Sharp's researches became more widely known, Fr George became one of his devoted associates. On leaving Thaxted he held church appointments in London and East Anglia and was vicar of Carbrooke, Norfolk for 22 years. Folk dancing became one of the flourishing parish activities and he arranged many Festivals and collected many traditional dances and songs in the county.

He was deeply interested in the relation of folk song and the early ecclesiastical plainchant which he had studied at Caldey and helped to introduce to Thaxted.

Fr George had a deep interest in all social movements to improve the lot of the working people. He was a consistent socialist and remained so to the end of his days and keenly supported all progressive movements in the world.

In his death we lose not only one of the pioneers of the folk revival and a champion of all oppressed people but a charming and devoted friend.

JACK PUTTERILL